This belongs to:-
Margaret Samuel

MILANESE LACE

MILANESE
LACE

An Introduction

Patricia Read and Lucy Kincaid

B.T. Batsford Ltd · London

First published 1988
© Patricia Read and Lucy Kincaid

ISBN 0 7134 5707 4

Phototypeset by Servis Filmsetting Ltd, Manchester
Printed in Great Britain by the Bath Press, Bath
for the publishers, B.T. Batsford Ltd,
4 Fitzhardinge Street, London W1H 0AH

*Milanese Braid Lace, designed and worked by Elsie
Vanstone. A circular mat – unfinished*

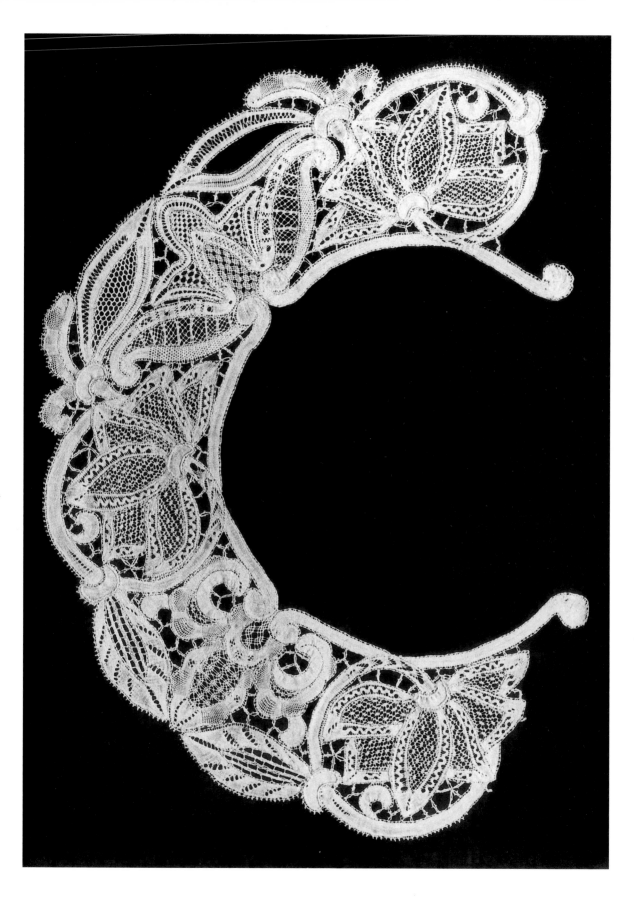

Contents

Acknowledgements

We would like to thank all those lace makers who helped us in the initial stages of our work on decorated braid, and especially those who have made lace for this book. Our special thanks to John Read who so patiently coped with our requests and produced such beautiful photographs. Our thanks to Eric Kincaid for his help with our original designs. Our acknowledgement to Aurora Art Publications, and to the Dover Pictorial Archive Series.

Introduction

I was taught lacemaking by Mrs Elsie Vanstone, who studied the craft with Margaret Maidment (author of *A Manual of Handmade Bobbin Lace*) at Battersea Polytechnic in the 1920s. Mrs Vanstone then became a lace teacher with the London County Council and had many classes in the south-east until she retired in 1964. Her fine work was always an inspiration to her students, not least to me. She encouraged me to start classes on my own and from 1949 I have worked as a lace tutor for the L.C.C. now ILEA. In 1953 Mrs Vanstone became my mother-in-law. My mother also made lace and I am very proud that my daughter is continuing the family tradition. I was very fortunate to have access to Mrs Vanstone's store of patterns, books and expertise at a time when there was no market for the lace books available to us today. The frontispiece shows a design of Mrs Vanstone's worked by herself: it has ever been my ambition to emulate this.

My students and I have studied old lace in museums, private collections and books and we came to the conclusion that whereas a pattern in lace such as torchon and Bucks Point is the same whoever works it, decorated braids though con-forming to broad traditions are very inventive and bear very closely the hallmarks of the individual worker/designer.

A great deal of interesting and varied new work followed an experimental period trying out the different braids. Having worked for so long with the traditional approach to lacemaking, I have tended to stay with the old styles of design (Chapter Five). Lucy, on the other hand, has shown less inhibition and has developed a modern approach which is attractive and worthwhile both from the design point of view and its technical interest (Chapter Six). This book is a collection of our formulae for working the braids and some of the patterns which we have designed and worked. We hope these will be an inspiration to other lacemakers who, like us, have worked through the Torchon, Beds, Bucks and Honiton traditions and are still looking for pastures new. More than that, it should lead to the creation of individual work.

At one of the A.G.M.'s of the Lace Guild it was asked 'Where is lace going?' We hope this will be one of the pathways for you to explore.

Patricia Read

CHAPTER 1

Preparation

Equipment

There are various items necessary for making bobbin lace, most of which can be home-made fairly cheaply and satisfactorily. There is, however, a list of mail order suppliers at the back of the book and it is recommended that you obtain their stock lists.

All equipment should be kept clean and tidy. A pincushion filled with emery dust will keep pins smooth and sharp. Protect needle pins and prickers with small pieces of cork. Keep a few drawing pins in the pricking board. A see-through six inch plastic ruler as a guide for pricking should be kept in the work-box, also a small piece of fine sandpaper to smooth any roughness on bobbins.

Pillow

A good quality pillow is essential. For decorated braids, a mushroom pillow, only slightly domed, is recommended. To make such a pillow you will need:

A piece of board or plywood cut in a circle 46cm in diameter.
A quantity of hay or straw, roughly chopped.
A strong sewing needle or packing needle, and thread
Two circles of tough, non-stretch fabric cut 51cm in diameter.

TO ASSEMBLE:
Machine stitch the two circles of material with a one inch hem, half-way round the circle. Turn inside out and insert the board, which should only just fit, with no slackness in the material. Turn in, pin, and hand-stitch a one inch hem for a quarter of the circle, leaving the remaining quarter open. Stuff the cavity (on one side of the board only) until it is packed very firmly, banging it and/or using a mallet. Turn in, pin and hand-stitch the last hem, closing the cavity.

The quality of your lace depends upon the absolute firmness of the pillow. Any hollow spaces will not hold the pins used in the making of the lace and slack tension and possible distortion will result.

Cover Cloths

Several are required and need to be kept regularly laundered. Preferably they should be plain, non-stretch fabric and of some pleasant colour which is restful to the eyes, does not reflect the light (as does white) and will show up the light coloured threads that are used in making the lace. Dark green or blue is very good. One cover should be used over the bare pillow. This may be hemmed and a draw-string inserted. Others should be used to cover the edges of the pattern and another to cover the pillow when not in use. Pieces of clear acetate are useful to cover the lace as it progresses. They give visibility yet protect threads from pinheads as the work is turned. The edges of the acetate should not be sharp or they will wear the thread.

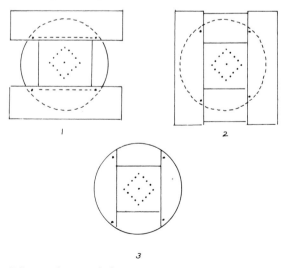

Pillow with cover cloths in position

Bobbins

Thirty-six will be sufficient for most of the patterns in this book. Fine English bobbins may be used. Many 'sewings' are taken in decorated braid patterns, therefore neatly wired, small spangles are necessary in order to avoid catching, and possibly breaking the thread. Other types of bobbins may be used, but spangled bobbins have the advantage of extra weight which prevents the thread from unravelling.

A spangled bobbin

A bobbin bag is a useful accessory. This is made by folding lengthwise a strip of material 60cm by 30cm and making stitch lines at 4cm intervals, giving pockets into which a pair of bobbins can be slipped and kept separately. See diagram.

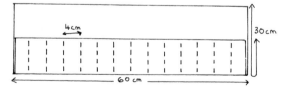

Pins

Short, fine, yellow or white brass pins are recommended. For braid lace, as for Honiton and other 'free' laces, the pins are pressed into the pattern as the work is turned. Long pins will bend. Keep a small supply of strong steel pins for pinning the pattern to the pillow and for fixing cover cloths. Berry or bead-headed pins should not be used.

Patterns

A supply of pricking card for pattern making is required. Prickings are prepared by taking a tracing or photocopy of the dotted pattern. This is secured with drawing pins over pricking card on to a cork or thick polystyrene base. The dots are then pricked with a pricker. A fine, black, waterproof marker pen should be used to draw in the pattern markings. If necessary, a pencil may be used first to mark the pattern but this must be done very lightly and the pencil marks rubbed out afterwards.

Tools

a) A *pricker* can be a small pin vice, obtainable from a good tool shop, with a Sharps needle, size seven, inserted. For finer holes use size eight or nine. Alternatively a needle may be inserted into a hard-topped cork or a short piece of dowelling with a hole drilled for the purpose, in which case the needle should be strongly glued into place. In all cases only about 15mm of the pointed end of the needle should be left protruding. Whilst pricking, the tool should be kept upright. Removing the pricker with a twist or sideways movement may snap the needle tip. In due course, the needles will blunt, and should be replaced occasionally. It helps if the needle is dipped in beeswax whilst pricking
b) *Fine pointed sharp scissors*
c) *Fine needle pin* for sewings (not to be used as a pricker)
d) *Fine crochet hook*, also used for sewings
e) *An inverted needle*, threaded with a loop of thread, is useful for difficult sewings
f) *A pin-pusher/lifter*

Threads

The thread used for the patterns in this book is given in each set of working notes. There is a variety of fine threads available, many of which are suitable for braid work. It is advisable to try a small sample of braid if it is intended to use a thread which is different from that recommended for a particular pattern. It may be necessary to adjust the number of bobbins used: more for a thread which is too fine and less for a thicker thread. Please note that for some of the decorated braids there is a set number of pairs to be used. In this case the only possible adjustment can be in the number of straight passive pairs inside the footing. Again, if in doubt work a small sample. For those workers who may have eyesight problems, the patterns can be enlarged and thicker thread used. This can be particularly successful with the modern designs in Chapter Six.

Notebook

Keep a notebook for your own notes and diagrams, as it is often necessary to refer back to what has been done at certain points.

Beginner's braid

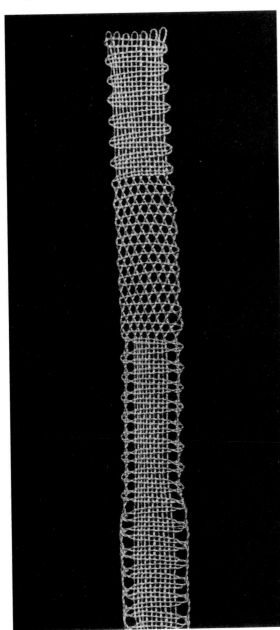

Pattern no. 1

Preparation

Wind up eight pairs of bobbins with Filato di Cantu No. 30 (or a thread of equivalent thickness).

To wind the bobbins:
> Hold one bobbin in the left hand and wind the thread in a clockwise direction.
> Cut the thread and wind back some of this thread on to the second bobbin. This gives a pair of wound bobbins. The thread is attached to the neck of the bobbin with a slip knot which is made as follows:
> Hold the bobbin in the left hand. With the right hand, hold the thread coming from the bobbin and wind it round the neck of the bobbin three times. Keeping it in position with the thumb of the left hand, pull up the thread to tighten.

Prick pattern number one and pin it down at the four corners on to the pillow. Place the cover cloth across the lower half of the pattern.

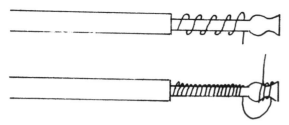

Setting up

Stick pins in the seven holes across the top of the pattern and hang one pair of bobbins on each pin. These seven pairs are called passives or down-rights. (See diagram.) The eighth pair is set up at pinhole (a) and will be the weavers (also called workers or leaders). This is the pair which will be worked from side to side through each of the passive pairs in turn.

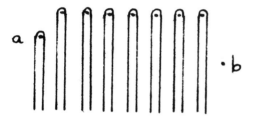

Stitches

There are two basic stitches to be learnt: cloth stitch (also called whole stitch) and half stitch. Other stitches are formed from the basic movements of these two stitches. Therefore it is essential for the beginner to become proficient in these movements so that the hands move fluently and automatically.

Cloth (or Whole) Stitch

This has three movements. Using the leaders and the first pair of passives work as follows:

First movement (with left hand)
cross
(one to the right)

Second movement (use both hands at the same time)
turn
(two to the left)

Third movement (with left hand)
cross
(one to the right)

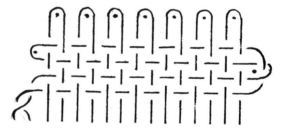

It will be seen that the weavers have changed places with the passive pair. The weavers now work the same stitch with the second pair of passives, and continue in the same manner until the weavers have worked through all the passive pairs to the end of the row.

The weavers are twisted twice towards the left (as in the second movement) and a pin is placed under the weaver threads and into the top hole (b), slanting slightly outwards and backwards in order to take the pull of the weaver threads. Gently pull down the passive bobbins whilst holding the weavers firmly to keep good tension and make the work flat and even. The beginner may find it helpful to say the words 'cross – turn – cross' as each movement is made and for speed in note taking x t x is a useful abbreviation of these movements. This abbreviation is used in some of the working notes later on in the book.

The weavers work back to the opposite side using *exactly* the same movements, working through each passive pair in turn. Again, at the end of the row twist the weavers twice towards the left (as in the second movement) and pin up. (See diagram.) Continue in this manner until about 10cm have been worked.

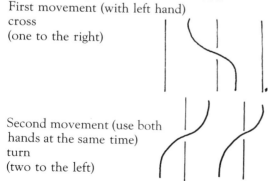

Half Stitch

This is made with the first two movements only, ie cross – turn (x t). When making this stitch it will be noticed that only one thread crosses from side to side and that the passive pairs are twisted. This is correct. The weavers should be twisted once at the end of each row, in addition to the twist which has been formed by the half stitch. (See diagram.) When changing the braid from cloth stitch to half stitch, the passive pairs should each be twisted right over left before commencing the first row of half stitch.

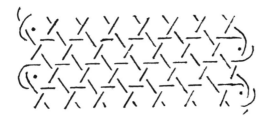

Edge Stitch – One

This will give a firm edge to the work with a picot effect. Work the weavers through the passive pairs in cloth stitch until one pair remains. Twist the weavers once, work through the last pair in cloth stitch, twist once the pair just worked through, twist the weavers twice, pin up. Close the pin with cloth stitch and twist both pairs once. (See diagram.)

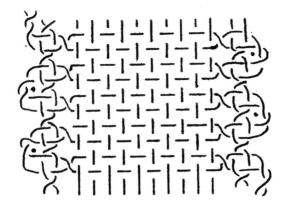

Edge Stitch – Two

This gives a straight edge which is suitable for mounting lace on to material. Work the weavers

through the passive pairs until one pair remains. Twist the weavers twice, work the weavers and the remaining pair in cloth stitch, twist both pairs twice. The pin is placed under the threads of both these pairs. The inside pair becomes the new weavers and work the next row across. The old weavers remain at the edge. (See diagram.)

Both sides of the braid may be worked with this edge stitch (sometimes called footing). Alternatively, one side may be worked with edge stitch one and the other side with edge stitch two. When either edge stitch is worked on half stitch braid, the weavers are not twisted before the last pair is worked because they are already twisted from the movement of the half stitch.

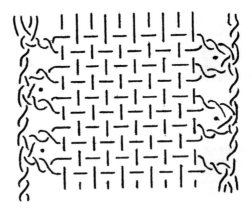

Sewings

Braids are connected by sewings. Sewings are made on the pillow while work is in progress, using a needle-pin, a threaded needle (it can be curved) or a fine crochet hook. For information on how these sewings are made see page 22.

CHAPTER 2

What is a Braid?

A braid is basically the same wherever it appears, whatever its length, breadth, or shape and whether it is decorated or not. It is always worked in the same way. It begins at one end, is worked along its length and is finished off at the other end. It can also be worked in a long continuous strip that twists and turns and many traditional braid patterns are made in this way. Alternatively, a number of braids can be joined together in the form of a jigsaw – a method frequently used in the more modern approach. Some 'jigsaws' incorporate short lengths of continuous braid within them.

A braid in Milanese lace does not have to be of uniform width throughout. Observe the differing widths and shapes of the braids in Chapter Six. As long as each shape is self-contained, that is, has its own beginning, middle and end, and is worked with a limited number of bobbins (usually less than 16 pairs) it qualifies as a braid.

Continuous braid

When working continuous braid it is necessary to negotiate tight bends and curves. There are several ways to do this. In all cases the aim is to keep the fabric smooth and not to allow it to bunch up on the inside of the curve or bend.

Ways in which to negotiate bends and curves

METHOD 1

If the curve is fairly gentle, it is possible to get round it with a succession of 'blind' pins. (See page 145.) Alternatively, drop the weavers as a passive on the inside of the curve and take the last pair of passives passed through as the new weavers. Take care not to pull the old weavers until they are worked into the braid, otherwise a hole will appear.

METHOD 2

Use the scroll method as described later in this chapter. This is most satisfactory on acute bends which seem to turn in on themselves, almost like a scroll or knob in a continuous braid.

METHOD 3

For sharp bends which are almost pointed, prick holes well into the point and leave one or two pairs at each pin as the work goes into the point, using the last pin several times, if necessary. Turn the pillow after the point has been reached, then as the work continues add in the pairs left at each pin, taking the pin out and using it again but taking care not to re-pin the previous loop. Pull up carefully each of the bobbins being taken in and the work will stay flat and close. Alternatively, it is possible to make a feature of this type of bend by making small plaits with each of the two pairs left out and making a decorative division as can be seen on the square mat on page 77.

A jigsaw of braids

A completely continuous braid has only one beginning and one end and is relatively straightforward to work. A 'jigsaw' of braids in which there are a number of beginnings and endings is not so simple and there are certain matters one *must* consider before work can start.
a) Whereabouts in the jigsaw to start.
b) Which end of a braid to start.
c) Different ways to begin a braid. This is determined by the position of the braid in the jigsaw.
d) Different ways to finish a braid. This too is determined by its position in the jigsaw.
e) How to join braids together.

Whereabouts in the jigsaw to start

Study the design carefully. Look for the key

braids, ie those onto which other braids can be joined, either as they begin, or as they finish (for example, the belt on page 103 where both the bodice and the skirt can work towards the belt). Once the key pieces have been worked, other pieces follow naturally. There may be more than one place in a pattern to start. The photographs and notes in Chapters Five and Six will help you reach an understanding of how these jigsaws are put together, and the order in which the braids are worked. The same basic principles apply to every design.

Beginning a braid

Which end of a braid to start?

This depends on the position of the braid in the design, if, and where, it is joined to another, and if other braids are joined to it. You must decide this yourself.

As a practice exercise, trace the lines of a pricking, then work out the sequence in which the braids are worked. Look at each braid separately, deciding where it is joined to another, how it is started and finished and which direction it is worked in. It is worth taking the time to make a tracing like this every time you work a pattern since it can show you more clearly than a whole page full of words exactly what is happening.

Beginning a braid where it is attached to another piece of the work

This is done by sewing in. Decide how many pairs the braid requires. This depends on the decoration and width of the braid. Count the number of pinholes available for the sewings. Divide the number of pairs between the number of holes, taking care to keep the outside pairs lined up with the edge of the new braid. Sew the pairs in. *Replace the pins.*

The weaver starts on the opposite side to the first pinhole. x t x t t (abbreviations on page 24) the two outside pairs together. Leave the outside pair as the edge pair. Take the second pair across as the weavers and proceed in the usual way.

Beginning at a point

Hang six pairs on a pin. (See page 146.) Twist all pairs twice. Decide which pinhole is worked first. This is the hole nearest to the one around which

Which end of a braid to start?

the pairs have been hung. Take the two pairs on the *opposite* side to the first pinhole. x t x t t them together. Leave the outside pair. Take the next pair through as the weavers until one pair remains. Twist the weavers twice. Work the weavers and the remaining passive pair together to make the usual edge stitch. Pin under two pairs. Close the pin and continue, laying in pairs as the work widens. (See page 144.)

17

Beginning with a false footing

This is used when the end of the braid is 'free', as at the edge of a skirt, or when another braid is to be sewn into it later on. It may be necessary to put in extra pinholes to get the required number of pairs. Count the number of pinholes in the false footing row. Allow two pairs for every hole.

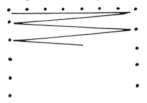

Decide which pinhole is the first to be worked after the false footing row is finished and start the false footing at this end. (Left in the diagram.)

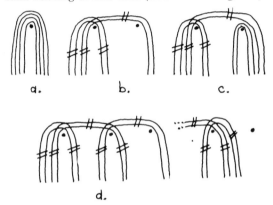

a.   b.   c.

d.

Hang four pairs round the first pin. x t x t t the two pairs on the left of the pin. Twist the two pairs on the right of the pin twice each. Put the next pin (the second) under the pair on the extreme right. Leave this pair. Hang two more pairs round this *same* pin (the second), keeping the pair already round the pin, to the extreme right. Twist the pair on the left of the pin, twice. x t x t t the two pairs on the right of the pin together. Put the next pin (the third) under the pair on the extreme right. Continue in this way until two pinholes remain to be worked. At the second to last pinhole proceed as before but do not pin under the pair on the extreme right. Leave the last pinhole unworked. Go back to the left side. Take the second pair from the end as the weavers and work all the way across until one pair remains. Twist the weavers and work the usual edge stitch with the weavers and this remaining pair. Put a pin in the last (unworked) hole of the false footing row, under two pairs. Close the pin, proceed as usual. If the false footing is started on the right side, reverse left and right in the instructions.

Using a false footing to make an angled edge

Work the corner pinhole where the two angles meet, laying in one pair. Return the weavers to the opposite edge and leave for the time being. Put pin one under the existing edge pair and in the first hole of the angled edge. Hang two pairs round this pin. Twist the pair on the right. x t x t t the two pairs on the left, then proceed in the usual way for a false footing, using the weaver pair left at the edge to work the first row.

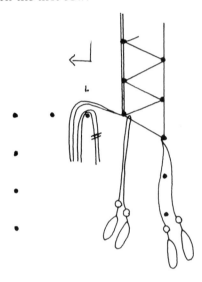

Beginning a braid with pairs left from another braid

Pairs can be carried straight from one braid to another if the design allows it, as in the bonnet on page 102. Here one braid makes a 'u' turn into another. Decisions of this kind are at the discretion of the worker.

Beginning in the middle of a braid

When there is a join in a braid, such as in the frame of the mermaid pricking, prick a row of holes across the braid. Hang two pairs round the outside pin. The other pairs are shared between the remaining pins and hung side by side (see page 146). Twist the two pairs on the outside pin twice, then work them together x t x t t. Take the second pair as the weavers and continue as usual.

Beginning with a scroll

See page 20.

Finishing a braid

Finishing when the braid is to be attached to another that has already been worked

This is done by sewing off. Work the last hole, take the weavers across to the opposite side, through all except the edge pair. Count the number of pairs. Count the number of holes available for sewing into. Divide the number of pairs between the number of holes, taking care not to distort any element of the decoration. Sew the pairs into the holes, sewing the weavers first. It is not always necessary to sew in all the pairs: use your own judgement. If unsure which pinhole to sew into, check by lifting the pin slightly and holding the pair against it.

Always put the pins back. This gives a firm anchorage against which to pull the pair as it is tied. Do not tie the threads until you are sure the pairs are in the right place. If a thread breaks while tying, tie its partner to another lying alongside it.

Sewing off into an awkward shape

Concentrate on keeping the path of the weavers correct, if necessary either missing a hole, or sewing into a hole twice. Each time the weavers are sewn in, lay some of the passives aside. How many depends on the shape itself and the decoration being worked. Judge this for yourself. When the weavers are sewn into the last hole, check the position of the passives and sew them into the appropriate holes. Tie all pairs and cut off.

Finishing at a point

Reduce the number of pairs as the braid gets narrow. (See page 144.) Proceed until three holes remain unworked. The fewer pairs that remain the better (a minimum of seven at this stage), but do not take out so many that the look of the braid is spoiled. Lay back one pair after each of the remaining three holes has been worked. Keep these separate to any others that have been laid back. When the last hole has been worked take the weavers through all pairs to the other side, without twisting and including the edge pair. Tie the weavers. Tie each of the remaining pairs. Take all pairs, except the two outside pairs of this bunch, in one hand. Cross the two remaining pairs, one over the other, under the bunch. Lay the bunch down on top of them. Tie the crossed pairs over the

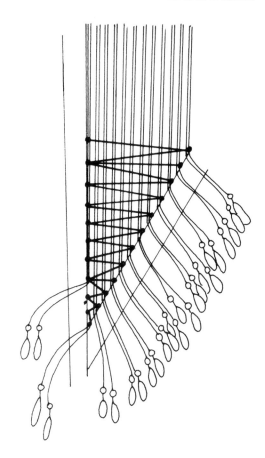

Sewing off into an awkward shape

bunch. Push down all pins, except the last two put in. Cut off all pairs laid back except the last three. Turn the pillow so that the bobbins lie away from you. Take the three pairs of threads which were laid aside. Open them out so that they lie inside one another. Take the bobbins in one hand, and keeping the threads taut, pull them between the two standing pins towards yourself. Lay them between the spread out pairs. Tie each of these pairs separately over the bunch. Cut all pairs off. This is known as bunching.

Finishing with a false footing

Try to ensure that there are two pairs for every hole available in the false footing row. Put in more holes if necessary. If finishing on the right, read right for left in the instructions. Work to the last hole on the left. Make the edge stitch. Work back through two passive pairs. The last pair worked through becomes the new weaver. Return with it to the edge and work the edge stitch.

* Work back through four passive pairs. Lay the

two pairs on the left of this group of four pairs, back across the pillow. Take the last pair worked through as the weavers and work back to the edge. Work the edge stitch. Repeat from * until the last pin has been set, but not closed, and four pairs remain (two edge, one weaver, one passive). Take these four pairs. Twist the passive pair twice and take it through the edge pair on the right. Cross the two centre pairs together x t x. Tie the two pairs on the right together. Tie the two pairs on the left together. If possible arrange it so that these four pairs can be carried into another piece of the work, or sewn off into an adjoining braid. If not, then proceed as follows: tie all thrown back pairs, and cut off all except two pairs nearest the corner. Lay these two pairs open. Bring the pairs tied at the corner and lay them between these two pairs. Tie these two pairs round the bunch twice. This should hold the four corner pairs out of sight when the work is turned over. Cut off all pairs.

Finishing in the middle of a braid

Sew the pairs into the loops which were made when the braid was begun.

Finishing with a scroll

See page 21.

Scroll sample

This sample is worked in cloth stitch. The same method applies for a half stitch scroll.
14 pairs wound with Copley Marshall No. 80 (or an equivalent thread).

To begin the scroll

Hang 6 pairs open on the third pin. (See page 146.) Make a cloth stitch with the 2 left pairs, twist these 2 pairs twice and the 2 right pairs. Take the second pair from the right as weavers and work to the left in cloth stitch through 3 pairs, twist weavers twice, slide new pair under weavers and leave at the back of the pillow. Make edge stitch with weavers and edge pair, pin under 2 pairs, bring down the new pair from the back of the pillow and place to the left of the passive pairs. Take another new pair and slide under the weavers (second pair from left) and leave at the back of the pillow.

Work weavers through 1 pair and tie one knot on the weavers to keep the work from pulling away from the pin. Work weavers through 3 more pairs, twist weavers twice, slide new pair under weavers and leave at back of pillow. Work edge stitch with weavers and edge pair, pin under two pairs.

Bring down the 2 pairs from the back of the pillow, one on the right and one on the left of the passives. They should be brought down carefully inside the pins. Slide a new pair under the weavers and leave at the back of the pillow. Work weavers through one pair and tie one knot with the weavers. Work weavers through all passives, twist twice, slide a new pair under the weavers and leave at the back of the pillow. Make the edge stitch, pin under two pairs and bring down the two pairs from the back of the pillow, as before. Slide a new pair under the weavers, leave at back of pillow, work weavers through one pair and tie one knot, work weavers through passive pairs to right, twist weavers twice. Slide new pair under weavers, leave at back of pillow. Pin under weavers but do not work edge

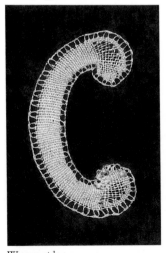
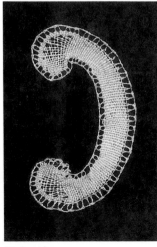
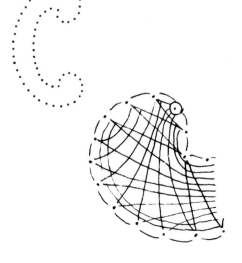

Wrong side   *Right side*

stitch as this will be a blind pin (or backstitch). Bring down the new pairs and place as before. Work weavers through all passives to left. Twist weavers twice and slide a new pair under weavers and leave at the back of pillow. Edge stitch and pin. Bring down the new pair, which is also the last new pair to be added, making a total of 14 pairs.

Scroll method

Work the weavers through one pair and tie one knot. Work the weavers through one more pair. Leave.

There are nine passive pairs to the right of the weavers. Number them from 1 to 9 from left to right.

Work no. 1 passives through 3 pairs to the left, twist twice, edge stitch and pin under 2 pairs. Work back through 2 pairs only. Leave.

Work no. 2 passives through 4 pairs to the left, twist twice, edge stitch and pin under 2 pairs. Work back through 2 pairs only. Leave.

Continue in this manner working
   no. 3 passive pair through 5 pairs to the left
   no. 4 passive pair through 6 pairs to the left
   no. 5 passive pair through 7 pairs to the left
   no. 6 passive pair through 8 pairs to the left
   each time working back from the edge stitch
   through 2 pairs only.

Work no. 7 passives through 9 pairs to the left, twist twice, edge stitch and pin under 2 pairs. Work back through all the passive pairs including nos. 8 and 9, twist twice, make the edge stitch, remove pin from the 'blind' hole and re-pin.

Continue working in cloth stitch braid, making 'blind' pins as necessary to keep the work level.

To end with a scroll

When pinhole X is reached, make a blind pin. There should be eleven pinholes remaining to be worked.

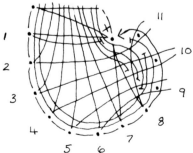

Work the weavers from pinhole X to pinhole 1. Work the weavers from pinhold 1 through all the passive pairs and throw it out (ie place it to the back of the pillow). Take the third passive pair from the left as new weavers and work to the left through 2 pairs, twist twice, edge stitch and pin. Work back through 2 pairs. Leave. The next five passive pairs to the right of these weavers should be numbered 1 to 5 from left to right (the remaining 3 passives need not be numbered).

Take no. 1 passive pair as new weavers and work to the left through 3 pairs, twist twice, edge stitch and pin under 2 pairs. Work back through 2 pairs only. Leave. Continue in this manner working
   no. 2 passive pair through 4 pairs to the left
   no. 3 passive pair through 5 pairs to the left
   no. 4 passive pair through 6 pairs to the left
   each time working back through 2 pairs only.

Work no. 5 passive pair as new weavers through 7 pairs to the left, twist twice, edge stitch and pin. Work back through all pairs and make up the blind pin. Work weavers across to the left through all pairs, twist twice, edge stitch and pin under 2 pairs. There should now be 3 holes remaining to be worked. Set aside the second and third passive pairs from the right. These will be used to tie back the last few pairs, so do not let them get muddled with other pairs.

Work the weavers through all the passive pairs to the right. Leave. Take the last pair passed through and work it to the left through 5 pairs and throw it out. Work the second passive pair from the left through 5 pairs to the right and throw it out. Work the first passive pair from the left through 4 pairs and throw it out.

There should now be, in this order: 1 edge pair, 6 passive pairs and 1 edge pair.

Twist the 6 passive pairs twice each and pin between each set of 2 passives in the last 3 holes. Work the left edge pair through these 6 pairs, twisting twice between each set of 2 pairs. Make a cloth stitch with the 2 edge pairs. Pull up well and knot each of these 2 pairs three times.

The last 6 pairs: Knot the left pair twice, place this pair between the next pair which should then be knotted twice over it. Take one of these bobbins and one bobbin from the laid-in pair and knot twice, repeat with the other two bobbins and throw out the laid-in pair. Repeat this process with the next 4 pairs but do not throw out the last pair. There are now 2 pairs and 2 edge pairs remaining. Leave these four pairs. Cut closely all the thrown out pairs. Turn the pillow. Separate the 2 pairs which were set aside specially for tying back and place the bundle of 4 pairs between them. Knot the 2 pairs over the bundle, using double threads. Knot twice each of the pairs in the bundle. Cut all pairs closely.

Decorated scroll

A scroll can have an added interest by working a 4-pin or 6-pin bud (see Leaves, page 78).

The opening row for the bud should start on completion of the scroll method when the last passive pair is taken as a new weaver.

Joining braids together

Joining two braids which run side by side and have a row of holes in common

The first braid is worked as usual with a footing on both sides. The second braid is worked with a footing on the outside edge only. Each time the weavers meet the point at which the two braids touch, the pin in the first braid is removed and the weavers of the second braid sewn into the pinhole. The pin is then replaced and the weavers returned to the outside edge.

Joining two braids when both have a footing on both sides

The first braid is worked normally. As the second braid is worked alongside it and the weavers come to the point where the two braids meet, proceed as follows: twist the weavers twice. Make the edge stitch but do not twist the pairs. Put the pin in. Now the appropriate pin is removed from the adjacent braid. The nearest pair to it, is sewn into this hole and the pin put back. This pair now works x t x t t with the pair it left behind at the pin in its own braid and is carried back into the work as the weavers.

Joining braids when there is a gap between them

There is a variety of ways to do this. They are explained in detail in Chapter Four.

Sewings

Work to the pinhole where the pair is to be sewn in and remove the pin. Make sure the pair is twisted or not twisted, according to the stitch being used. Take one thread of the pair and pull it through the loop at the pinhole. Pass the second bobbin through the loop just made. Pull up the loop. *Put the pin back.* Continue with the work.

Top sewings

A top sewing is made when the first loop is pulled round the side bar of the pinhole loop. More than one sewing can be made round each bar if necessary. A *top sewing* has the effect of creating a small ridge along the edge of the braid on the right side of the work. It can create the illusion of one braid being in front of another, i.e. hair in front of a face. In order to achieve this effect, the braid which appears to be on top when the work is finished *must* be worked first. In a complicated design this needs some careful thought. Remember, you are working with the wrong side of the work towards you. When the work is turned over, if top sewings have been used, the braid which was worked first will appear to be on top. This is a simple rule to follow once you have convinced yourself it works.

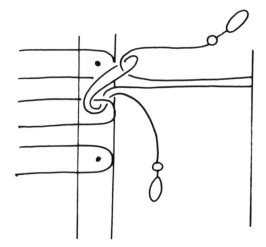

Edge sewings

An edge sewing is made when the first loop is pulled round the front edge of the pinhole loop. This has the effect of making the edges of the braid butt instead of overlap. It does not matter which order the braids are worked in when doing edge sewings.

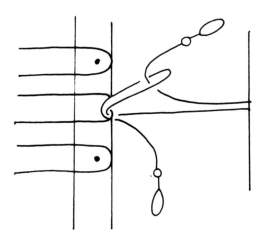

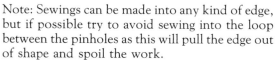

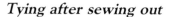

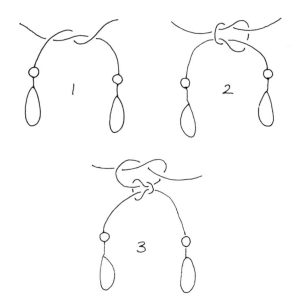

Note: Sewings can be made into any kind of edge, but if possible try to avoid sewing into the loop between the pinholes as this will pull the edge out of shape and spoil the work.

Tying after sewing out

Before a sewn out pair is cut off, it must be tied. Do this with a reef knot followed by half a reef knot. Three movements in all. Left over right. Right over left. Left over right. Make sure each stage of the knot is pulled up close to the work with no gaps between.

CHAPTER 3

Decorated Braids

If this particular form of braid work has not been attempted before, it is recommended that a few samples should be worked before starting a pattern. Suggestions for a first selection include Basketweave, Archway, Meander-in-Braid (variation one), Ovals, and perhaps some buds and divisions. If the samples are made about 8 cms long, they are useful for reference when choosing a braid for a particular section or shape in a pattern. It will be noticed that some braids are more open (Archway) and others have a very close texture (Basketweave). The following patterns are given in alphabetical order.

Abbreviations used in the patterns:

pr prs	pair, pairs
lt	left
rt	right
W	Weaver, workers or leaders
thro	through
tw	twist
cls	cloth (or whole) stitch
hs	half stitch
Rpt	repeat
* ts	* turning stitch
st	stitch
x t	cross – turn (half stitch)
x t x	cross – turn – cross (whole, or cloth, stitch)
x t t	cross – turn – turn

* turning stitch has been indicated on the diagrams by a circle (o)

Turning Stitch

This is often used in the deliberate making of holes and for a weaver which has to turn in the work but has no pinhole to support it. It is also used to divide a braid, thus giving two weaver pairs. There are several ways of making a turning stitch. Throughout the patterns in this book the following method has been used:

cross – turn – cross – turn – cross

that is, two half stitches then cross the two centre bobbins left over right. (Remember the five movements by the five fingers on one hand.)

It will be seen from the diagram that one thread of each pair changes places and becomes part of the opposite pair. Other methods may be used if found to be satisfactory.

Tension

It will be seen that the only pinholes are at the sides of the braid and that pins are seldom used in the making of the decorated part of the braid, even as support pins. Pulling the bobbins too hard can sometimes distort the work, therefore great care must be taken to ease the threads into position. Good tension is important and the skill of the lacemaker is paramount.

Angels

14 prs

Ts with W and centre pr.

Lt W cls to lt thro 5 prs, tw W twice, edge st and pin. Leave. Work rt W to rt in similar manner.

Centre 6 prs:
Tw each pr once.

* Centre 4 prs:
Cross 2 lt prs thro 2 rt prs in cls. Lt 2 prs work 1 cls and rt 2 prs also work 1 cls.

Left side:
W thro 2 prs, tw W once, cls and tw thro next pr, cls thro next pr, ts with next pr, return thro 1 pr, tw W once, cls and tw thro next pr, cls thro 2 prs, tw W twice, edge st and pin. W thro 1 pr in cls. Leave. Tw the next pr once.

Right side:
Work in similar manner to lt side.

Cross 2 centre lt prs thro 2 centre rt prs in cls.

Tw each of these 4 prs once.

Work the lt of these 4 prs to the lt in cls and tw thro 2 prs, cls thro 2 more prs, tw W twice, edge st and pin. W thro 1 pr in cls. Leave. Tw next pr once.

Work the centre lt pr to the lt in cls and tw thro 3 prs, cls thro 2 prs, tw W twice, edge st and pin.

Work the rt side in a similar manner. *

Rpt from * to * for desired length.

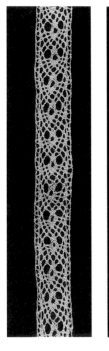
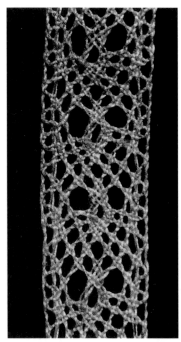

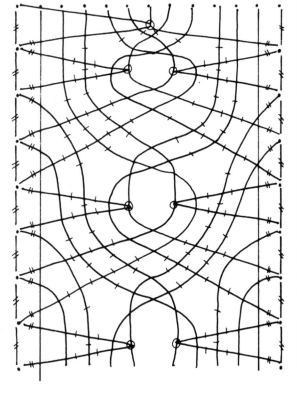

Archway

14 prs

* Ts with W and centre pr. Cls is used throughout.

Left side:
Work lt pr of the centre 2 prs thro 5 prs to lt, tw W twice, edge st and pin.

Work W thro 5 prs, leave W and take last pr passed thro as new W and return thro 4 prs, tw W twice, edge st and pin.

Work W thro 4 prs, leave W and take last pr passed thro as new W and return thro 3 prs, tw W twice, edge st and pin.

Work W thro 3 prs, leave W and take last pr passed thro as new W and return thro 2 prs, tw W twice, edge st and pin. Work W thro 2 prs. Leave.

Right side:
Work in similar manner to lt side.

Centre 8 prs:
Tw each pr 3 times.

Cross lt 4 prs thro rt 4 prs in ws.

New W will be the 2nd passive pr on the side of braid with next pinhole to be worked.

The pattern may be repeated from * but one or more rows of cls may be worked before the archway is repeated. In the sample shown 1 row of cls was worked.

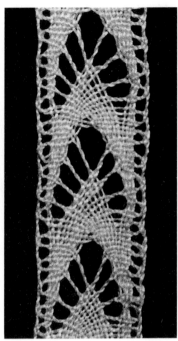

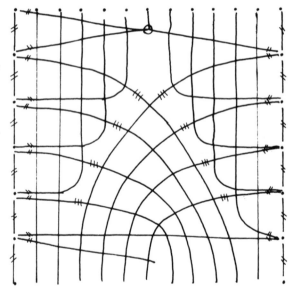

Basketweave

14 prs

Work 1 row of cls thro 11 prs, tw W twice, edge st and pin with last pr. Leave.

* Take next 2 passive prs, cls. Leave. Continue in this manner thro 8 more prs of passives, leaving 1 passive pr and edge pr unworked.

Work W thro in cls. Tw W twice, edge st and pin with last pr. Leave. *

Repeat from * to * for desired length.

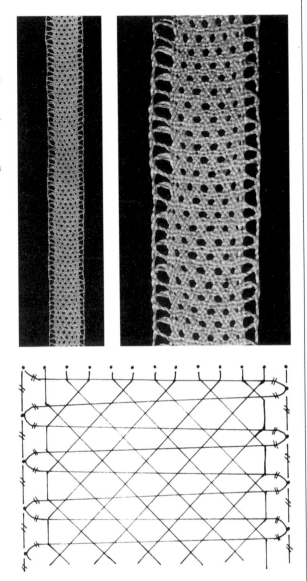

Beads

14 prs

Ts with W and centre pr. Both these pairs are weavers and they work in cls throughout.

Work lt W to lt thro 5 prs, tw W twice, edge st and pin. Leave.

Work rt W to rt in similar manner.

* Centre 4 prs:
Work 1 cls with 2 lt prs and 1 cls with 2 rt prs.

Cross the 2 lt prs thro the 2 rt prs in cls.

Work 1 cls with the 2 lt prs and 1 cls with the 2 rt prs.

Left side:
W thro 3 prs, tw W once, thro 1 more pr, ts with next pr. Return thro 1 pr, tw W once, thro 3 prs, tw. W twice, edge st and pin. Leave.

Right side:
Work in similar manner to lt side *

Rpt from * to * for desired length, finishing with the crossing of the 4 centre prs.

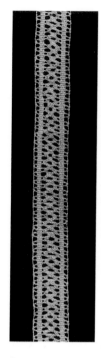
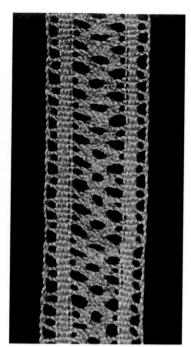

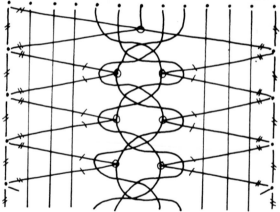

Buds

4-Pin Bud and 6-Pin Bud

14 prs

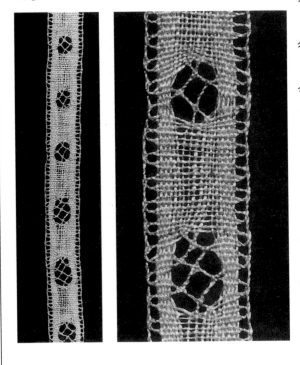

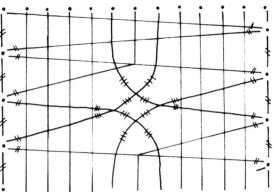

6-Pin Bud (made without pins)

Work from * to * as for 4-Pin Bud, and then from ** to **.

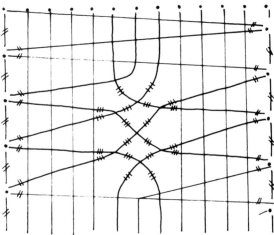

4-Pin Bud (made without pins)

In cls braid:
* W thro 7 prs, work last but one pr passed thro back thro 1 pr.

2 outside prs of these centre 4 prs are weavers.

2 centre prs: tw 3 times each, cls and tw 3 times. Leave.

** Work weavers to edges and back (but not thro) the centre twisted prs.

Tw weavers 3 times and work them to centre. Tw all 4 prs 3 times each.

2 outside prs of these centre 4 prs are now weavers.

2 centre prs: cls and tw 3 times. Leave. *

Work weavers to edges and back to centre, work cls with 2 centre prs (both weavers). Use pr nearest to next hole to be worked as new W. The other pr becomes a passive. **

Cloth Divisions 1

In cls braid:
Tw the passive prs 3 times.

All the passive prs may be twisted but if the braid is curved, only some of the passive prs on the outside of the curve need be twisted.

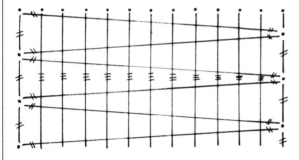

Cloth Divisions 2

14 prs
Leave W at the edge.

* Take next 2 passive prs and work cls and tw (called a 'double'). Rpt from * twice more.

Three 'doubles' have now been worked.

Tw twice next passive pr and work cls with this pr and first pr from the last 'double'. Leave.

** Work cls with the second pr from this 'double' and the first pr from the next 'double'. Leave.

Rpt from ** once more. Tw twice on the remaining pr.

Continue working with W.

If the braid is fairly wide, more 'doubles' can be made.

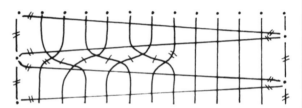

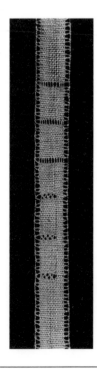
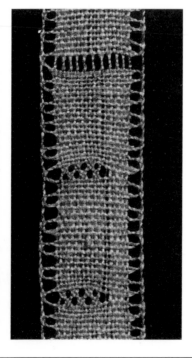

Cloth Divisions 3

14 prs

W works in cls throughout.

Work 2 rows.

Next row: work W thro 4 prs. Leave. Tw remaining 7 passive prs once each. Work W thro these 7 prs, twisting the W once between each pr, but do not tw the passive prs. Tw W twice, edge st and pin. Leave.

* Work next 2 prs in cls. Leave. Rpt from * twice more. Tw next pr once.

Work W thro 6 prs cls and tw. W thro next pr and tw passive pr once. W thro 4 prs, tw W twice, edge st and pin.

Continue working cls braid for desired length. In the sample shown there are eight rows of cls between the divisions.

The number of crossed pairs may be more or less according to the width and curve of the braid and the number of pairs used.

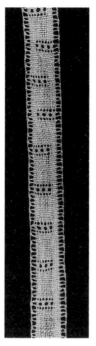
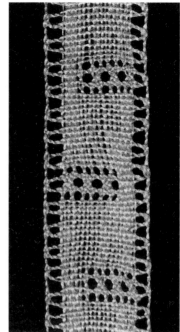

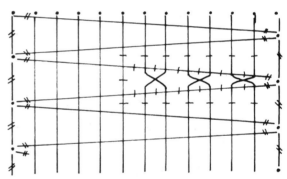

Crescent

14 prs

Ts with W and centre pr. Both these prs are now weavers and they work in cls throughout.

* Left side:
Work lt W to lt thro 3 prs, tw W twice, thro 2 more prs, tw W twice, edge st and pin.

Work W thro 2 prs, tw W twice, thro 1 more pr and ts with next pr. Return with W thro 1 pr, tw W twice, thro 2 more prs, tw W twice, edge st and pin. Leave.

Right side:
Work in similar manner to lt side.

Tw twice 6 centre prs.

Centre 4 prs:
Cross 2 lt prs thro 2 rt prs in cls and tw twice. Leave.

Left side:
Work W thro 2 prs, tw W twice, thro 1 more pr and ts with next pr. Return with W thro 1 pr, tw W twice, thro 2 prs, tw W twice, edge st and pin. Leave.

Right Side:
Work in similar manner to lt side.

Centre 6 prs (only the centre 2 prs having 2 tw). Cross lt 3 prs thro rt 3 prs in cls. No tw after the completion of this crossover.

Left side:
W thro 2 prs, tw W twice, thro 3 prs. Leave.

Right side:
W thro 2 prs, tw W twice, thro 4 prs.

The weavers have now changed sides. *

Rpt from * to * for desired length.

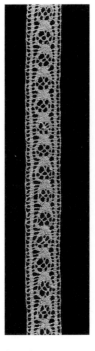
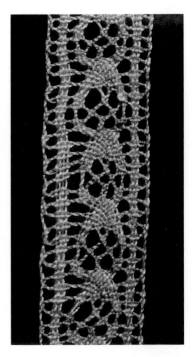
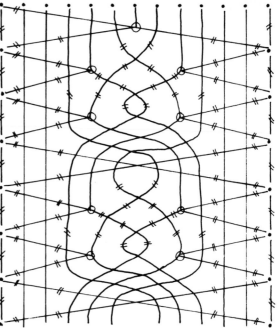

Cross-over 1

14 prs

Ts with W and centre pr. Both these prs are now weavers and they work in cls throughout.

Lt W thro 5 prs to lt, tw W twice, edge st and pin. Leave.

Work rt W to rt in similar manner. Leave.

** Left side:
W thro 2 prs, tw W once, cls and tw thro 1 pr, cls thro one more pr, ts with next pr, return thro 1 pr, tw W once, cls and tw thro 1 pr, cls thro 2 prs, tw W twice, edge st and pin. Leave.

Right side:
Work in similar manner to lt side.

Cross the 2 centre lt prs thro the 2 centre rt prs in cls.

Centre 6 prs:
Tw once each pr.

Lt pr cls and tw thro 2 prs to rt.

Rt pr cls and tw thro 3 prs to lt.

Left side:
* W thro 3 prs, ts with next pr, return to lt thro 3 prs, tw W twice, edge st and pin. Rpt from * once more.

Right side:
Work in similar manner to lt side.

Centre 6 prs:
Each pr twisted once.

Work centre lt pr cls and tw thro 2 prs to lt.

Work centre rt pr cls and tw thro 2 prs to rt.

Centre 4 prs:
Cross the 2 lt prs thro the 2 rt prs in cls. **

Rpt from ** to ** for desired length, finishing with the crossover of the centre 4 prs.

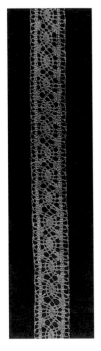
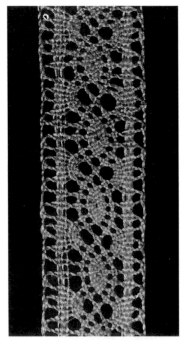
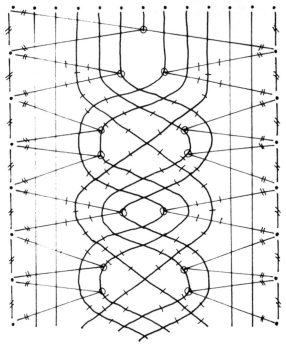

Cross-over 2

14 prs

Work 1 row of cls, edge st and pin. Leave.

Work one hs with 6th and 7th passive prs.

Work W in cls thro 5 prs, ts with next pr.

These two prs are now weavers and they work in cls throughout.

Work the lt W to the lt thro 5 prs, tw W twice, edge st and pin. Leave. Work the rt W to the rt in a similar manner. Leave.

† Centre 6 prs:
Tw once each.

Lt centre pr cls and tw thro lt 2 prs.
Rt centre pr cls and tw thro rt 2 prs.

Centre 4 prs:
Pass lt 2 prs thro rt 2 prs in cls.

Left side:
* Work W thro 2 prs, tw W once, cls and tw thro next pr, cls thro next pr, ts with next pr (put aside the remaining 7 prs). Return with W thro next pr, tw W once, cls and tw thro next pr, thro next 2 prs, tw W twice, edge st and pin.

Rpt from * once more. Leave.

Right side:
Work in similar manner to left side.

Centre 4 prs:
Cross 2 lt prs thro 2 rt prs.

Tw these 4 prs once.

Centre 6 prs:
The lt pr and the rt pr each work to centre in cls and tw thro 2 prs and thro each other and remain as the 2 centre prs (no twists on the other 4 prs).

Left side:
** Work W thro 3 prs, ts with next pr (put aside the remaining 8 prs). Return with W thro 3 prs, tw. W twice, edge st and pin.

Rpt from ** once more. Leave.

Right side:
Work in similar manner to lt side. †

To repeat the whole pattern work from † to †.

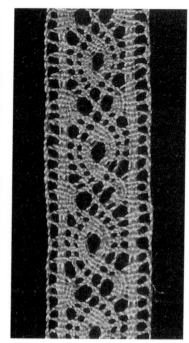
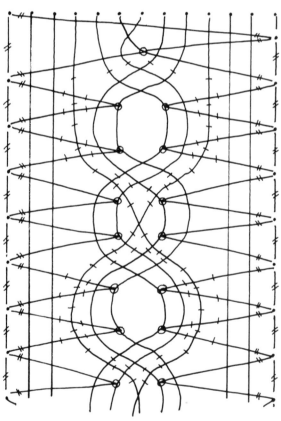

Figure-of-Eight 1

14 prs

Ts with W and centre pr. Both these prs are now weavers and they work in cls throughout.

Lt W work to lt thro 5 prs, tw W twice, edge st and pin.

Work rt W in similar manner on rt side.

** Centre 6 prs:
Cross lt 3 prs thro rt 3 prs in cls. Leave.

* Left side:
W thro 4 prs, ts with next pr, return thro 4 prs, tw W twice, edge st and pin.

Rpt from * once more. Leave.

Right side:
Work in similar manner to lt side.

Rpt from ** for desired length, finishing with the crossover.

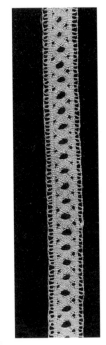
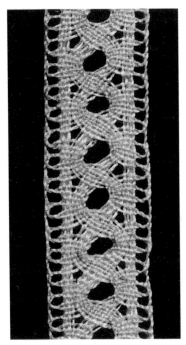

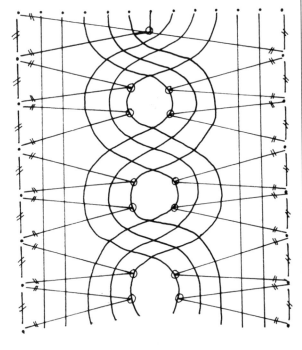

Figure-of-Eight 2

14 prs

Ts with W and centre pr. Both these prs are now weavers and they work in cls throughout.

Lt W work to lt thro 5 prs, tw W twice, edge st and pin.

Work rt W in similar manner on rt side.

** Centre 6 prs:
Ts each pr once and cross lt 3 prs thro rt 3 prs with cls and one tw. Leave.

Left side:
* W thro 4 prs, ts with next pr, return thro 4 prs, tw W twice, edge st and pin.

Rpt from * once more. Leave.

Right side:
Work in similar manner to lt side. **

Rpt from ** to ** for desired length, finishing with the crossover.

Note: In the crossover section, two twists may be used instead of one if using fine thread, or if pattern is slightly wider.

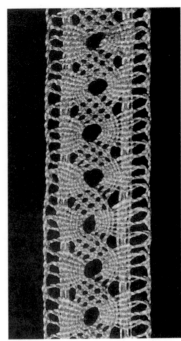

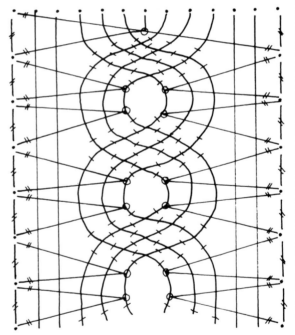

Figure-of-Eight 3

14 prs

Ts with W and centre pr. Both these prs are now weavers and they work in cls throughout.

Work lt W to lt thro 5 prs, tw W twice, edge st and pin. Leave.

Work rt W in similar manner on rt side. Leave.

** Centre 4 prs:
Tw each pr twice and cross lt 2 prs thro rt 2 prs in cls and tw twice. Leave.

Left side:
* Work W thro 3 prs, tw W twice, cls and tw twice thro next 2 prs. Leave W and return to lt with last pr passed thro as new W, cls and tw twice thro 1 pr, ws thro 3 prs, tw W twice, edge st and pin.

Rpt from * once more. Leave.

Right side:
Work in similar manner to lt side. Leave. **

Rpt from ** to ** for desired length, finishing with the crossover.

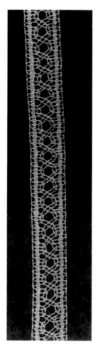
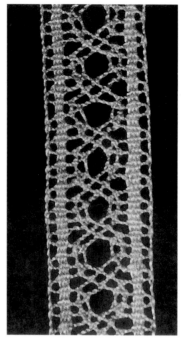

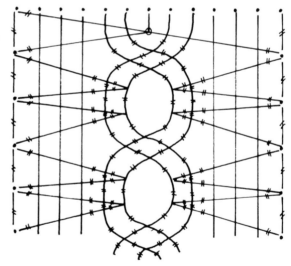

Fishes – with Two or Four Horizontals

13 prs

Weavers work in cls throughout.

† The fishes:
* Work W thro 2 prs, tw W once. Rpt from * to end of row, tw W once more, edge st and pin.

For 2 horizontals repeat this row once more.

For 4 horizontals repeat the row three more times.

The lattice work:
Leave W with the edge pr.

* Work cls and tw once with next 2 prs, leave.

Rpt from * to end of row, leaving the other edge pr unworked.

Work the W thro next pr in cls and tw. Leave.

** Work the next 2 prs in cls and tw. Leave.

Rpt from ** to end of row, including the edge pr, which should be twisted twice and pin up under 2 prs.

Work the inside pr of these last 2 prs with the next pr in cls. Leave. *** Work the next 2 prs in cls (no tw). Leave. Rpt from *** to last 2 prs.

Work edge st and pin with these last 2 prs.

Rpt from † for desired length.

Note: There are seven varieties of 'Fish' in *The Book of Bobbin Lace Stitches* by Bridget Cook and Geraldine Stott.

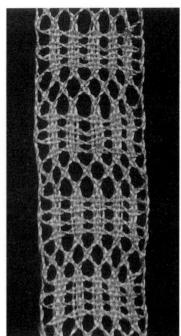
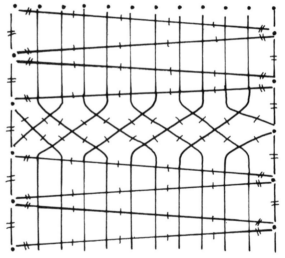

Haloed Fish

13 prs

† The fishes:
Work cls with 5th and 6th prs and with 9th and 10th prs.

* Work W in cls thro 1 pr, tw W once, cls and tw thro one pr, cls thro 2 prs, tw W once, cls and tw thro 2 prs, cls thro 2 prs, tw W once, cls and tw thro one pr, cls thro 1 pr, tw W twice, edge st and pin.

Rpt from * once more.

Work W thro 1 pr, tw W. Leave these 2 prs and edge pr.

Work cls and tw with 5th and 6th prs and with 9th and 10th prs.

Lattice work:

With 4 prs from first fish:
Cls and tw with 2 lt prs and same with the rt 2 prs. Leave.

With 4 prs from second fish:
Work in similar manner to first fish. Leave.

W and next pr: cls and tw. Leave. (Take the next 2 prs: cls and tw.) Rpt twice more, leave. Next pr thro 1 pr in cls, tw twice, edge st and pin. Return thro 1 pr, tw and work cls and tw thro next pr. Leave. (Take next 2 prs: cls and tw.) Rpt twice more, leave. Next pr thro 1 pr in cls, tw twice, edge st and pin. Leave.

Rpt from † for desired length, finishing with the lattice work.

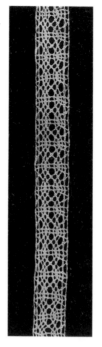
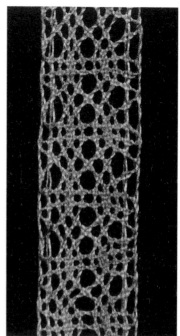

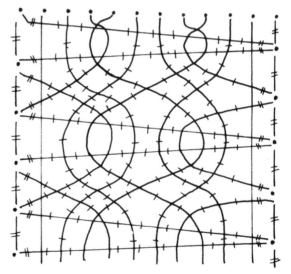

Hole 1

14 prs

To be worked in cls braid.

Leave W at edge.

Work hs with 5th and 6th passive prs.

Work W thro and make ts with W and the nearest of these two prs. W returns thro 4 prs, tw W twice, edge st and pin. Leave.

Other side: take remaining pr from hs as W and work thro 5 prs, tw W twice, edge st and pin.

Return thro 5 prs, tw W and next pr once and cross two centre bobbins lt over rt (a reverse hs).

Leave these two prs to become passives.

Continue braid with the original W.

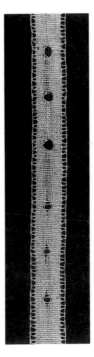
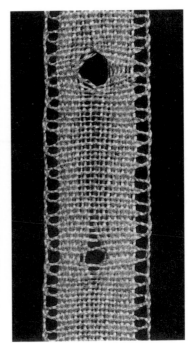

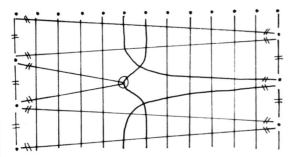

Hole 2

This gives a smaller hole than Hole 1.

Work W to where the hole is required, usually in the centre of the braid, tw W and last pr passed thro 3 times, work W thro next pr and tw this pr 3 times but not the W. Work W to end of row.

In the next row, the W only is twisted 3 times between the two twisted passive prs.

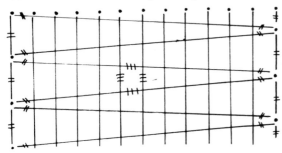

Horseshoe

14 prs

Ts with W and centre pr. Both these prs are now weavers and they work in cls throughout.

Work lt W to lt, thro 5 prs, tw W twice, edge st and pin. Leave.

Work rt W to rt in similar manner. Leave.

*Centre 6 prs tw each once and cross lt 3 prs thro rt 3 prs in cls.

Left side:
Work W thro 2 prs, tw W once, thro 2 more prs, ts with next pr (put aside remaining 7 prs), return thro 2 prs, tw W once, thro 2 prs, tw W twice, edge st and pin.

W thro 2 prs in cls, tw W once, thro 1 more pr, ts with next pr, return thro 1 pr, tw W once, thro 2 prs, tw W twice, edge st and pin.

Right side:
Work in similar manner to lt side. *

Rpt from * to * for the required length, finishing with the crossover.

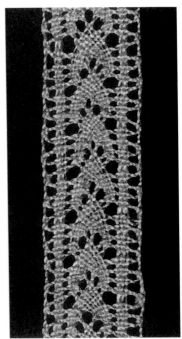

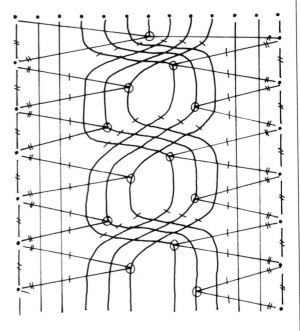

Italian Fish

13 prs

Work W thro one passive pr in cls, tw W once.

** The lattice work:

* Cross prs 4 and 5 thro prs 6 and 7 in cls.

Cross prs 8 and 9 thro prs 10 and 11 in cls. *

Tw these 8 prs once.

Cross the centre 4 prs in cls and tw.

Work pr 4 thro the W in cls and tw, then thro 1 pr, tw twice, edge st and pin. Return thro 1 pr, tw once. Leave.

Pr 5 also works thro to edge: thro 2 prs in cls and tw, thro 1 pr in cls, tw twice, edge st and pin.

Return thro 1 pr, tw once. This pr will become the W for the next set of fishes.

Work the opposite edge in a similar manner, using pr 11 first and then pr 10.

Rpt from * to * once.

The fishes:
† (W thro 2 prs, tw W once) 4 times, W thro 1 pr, tw W twice, edge st and pin. Return thro 1 pr, tw W once.

Rpt from † three more times.

Rpt from ** for desired length, finishing with the lattice work.

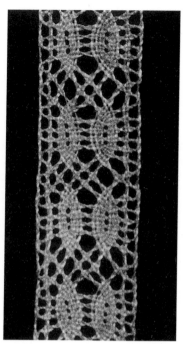

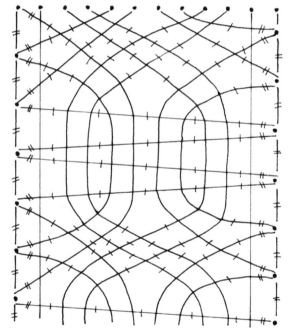

Jinks

14 prs

Ts with W and centre pr. Both these prs are now weavers and they work in cls throughout.

Work lt W thro 5 prs to lt, tw W twice, edge st and pin. Leave.

Work rt W to rt in similar manner. Leave.

Two centre prs: Cls and tw.

* Work lt W thro 5 prs to centre.

Work rt W thro 6 prs. The Ws have now changed sides.

Left side:
Work lt W thro 5 prs to lt, tw W twice, edge st and pin.

Work W thro 3 prs, ts with next pr, return thro 3 prs, tw W twice, edge st and pin. Leave.

Right side:
Work in similar manner to lt side. Leave.

Centre 4 prs:
Tw each pr once.

Cross lt 2 prs thro rt 2 prs in cls and tw once.*

Repeat from * to * for desired length.

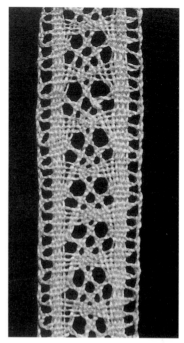

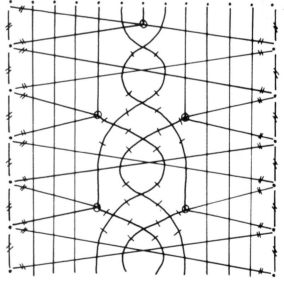

Kisses

13 prs

Work 2 rows in cls with edge st.

W works in cls throughout.

† Leave W and edge pr.

Centre 4 prs:
Cross 2 lt prs thro 2 rt prs in cls (no tw).

Tw once each of the 2 prs on the lt and 2 prs on the rt of the centre 4 prs.

Work W thro 1 pr, tw W once, thro 2 prs, tw once W and last 2 prs passed thro, W thro 2 prs, tw W once, thro 2 prs, tw W once, thro 2 prs, tw once W and last 2 prs passed thro, W thro 1 pr, tw W twice, edge st and pin.

* Work W thro 1 pr, (tw W once, W thro 2 prs) 4 times, tw W once, thro 1 pr, tw W twice, edge st and pin. *

Centre 8 prs:
Divide into 2 groups of 4 prs. Each group: lt pr tw once, 2 centre prs cls, rt pr tw once.

Rpt from * to * twice. †

To repeat the whole pattern work from † to †.

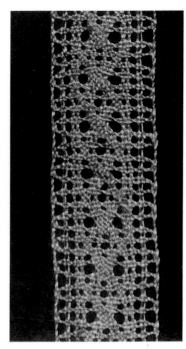

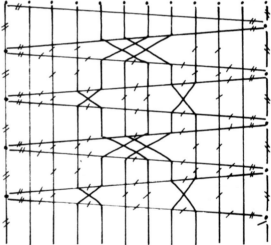

Lazy-Tongs

14 prs

Work in cls throughout.
Ts with W and centre pr. Work lt pr thro 5 prs to lt, tw W twice, edge st and pin, work back thro one pr. Leave.

Work rt side in similar manner.

* Centre 8 prs:
Tw each pr twice.

Cross 4 lt prs thro 4 rt prs.
Tw each pr twice.

Left side:
Work first pr (from centre 8 prs) thro 2 prs to lt (no tw). Leave.

Work 2nd pr thro 3 prs to lt, tw twice, edge st and pin, work back thro one pr. Leave.

Work 3rd pr thro 4 prs to lt. Leave.

Work 4th pr thro 5 prs to lt, tw twice, edge st and pin, work back thro 1 pr. Leave.

Right side:
Work in similar manner to left side.*

Rpt from * to *.

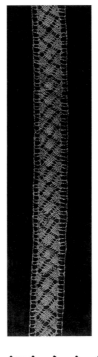
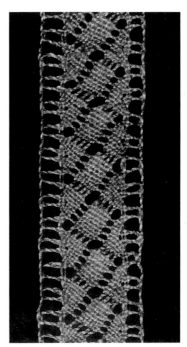

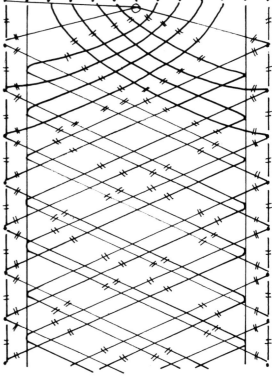

Little Spiders

14 prs

Ts with W and centre pr. Both prs work out to
their respective edges, close the pin and leave as the
second passive.

Centre 8 prs:
Lt 4 prs: pass the lt 2 prs thro the rt 2 prs in cls.
Work rt 4 prs in similar manner. *Tw twice 8 prs.
Lt 2 prs: work the first pr thro 2 prs to the lt in cls,
tw twice, edge st, pin, return thro 2 prs. Leave.
Work the second pr thro 3 prs to the lt in cls, tw
twice, edge st, pin, return thro 2 prs.

Rt 2 prs (of the 8 centre prs): work in similar
manner to the rt.

Centre 4 prs:
Work a cls spider, making a ts in the centre.

Centre 8 prs:
Tw twice each pr.

Work a cls spider with lt 4 prs.

Work a cls spider with rt 4 prts.

Rpt from * for desired length.

Note: A ts is made in the centre of the spiders and
no pin is used.

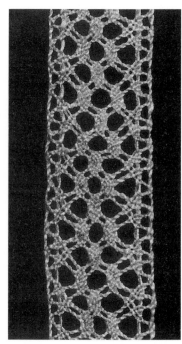

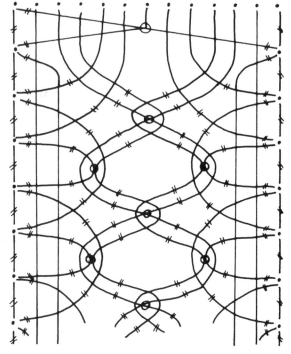

Maltese Spot

14 prs

In cls braid, make ts with W and centre pr. Both these prs are now weavers. Work the lt W to lt, thro 5 prs, tw W twice, edge st and pin. Leave. Work rt W to rt in similar manner.

Two centre prs: tw twice, cls.

Work lt W thro 4 prs, tw twice, cls thro next pr. Leave.

Work rt W thro 4 prs, tw twice, cls thro next pr.

Two weavers: cls. Weavers have now changed sides.

Lt W cls thro 1 pr, tw W twice, W thro 4 prs, tw twice, edge st and pin. Leave. Work rt W in similar manner.

Two centre prs: cls and tw twice.

Both weavers to centre and make ts. Of these two prs the one nearest the next hole to be worked is the W. The other pr remains as a passive.

Cross the 2 lt prs thro the 2 prs on the lt of them in cls.

Work the 2 rt prs (of the original centre 4 prs) in a similar manner to the rt.

Work both weavers to centre and work ts. Of these two prs the one nearest the next hole to be worked is the W. The other pr remains as a passive.

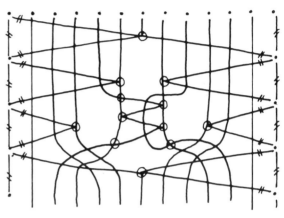

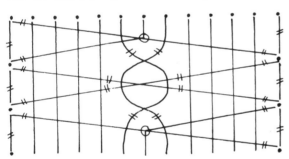

May Bud

In cls braid, make ts with W and centre pr. Both these prs are now weavers. Work lt W thro 5 prs to lt, tw W twice, edge st and pin. Work W thro 4 prs, ts with next pr, return thro 4 prs, tw W twice, edge st and pin. Work W thro 2 prs, ts with next pr, return thro 2 prs, tw W twice, edge st and pin. Leave. Work rt W to rt in similar manner.

Centre 4 prs:
Work cls with 2 rt prs.

Work ts with 2 lt prs. Taking the rt of these 2 prs, work backwards and forwards 4 times in cls and ts at each end. Finish with ts on lt. Leave.

Ts with 2 rt prs.

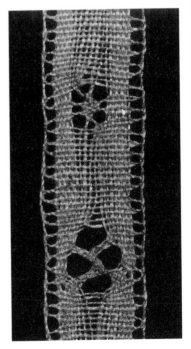

Meander-in-Braid 1

14 prs

Work 1 row of cls, make edge st and pin with last pr, tw both prs twice. Leave.

Make hs with 7th and 8th passive prs. Leave.

† * Work W in cls thro 3 prs, tw W twice, thro 3 more prs, and make ts with next pr (put aside the remaining 5 prs), return with W thro 3 prs, tw W twice, thro 3 more prs, tw W twice and make edge st and pin.

Repeat from * once more.

Leave edge pr, W and 3 passive prs. †

Other side:
Take remaining pr from hs as W, work ws thro 3 prs, tw W twice, edge st and pin, tw both prs twice.

Repeat from † to † as on first side.

Each side continues to work alternately.

To change to plain braid, work W thro 3 passive prs and make a reverse hs with W and next pr. To see this more clearly turn diagram upside down and note where passives 7 and 8 opened the braid.

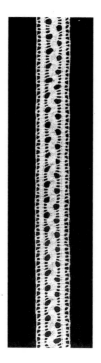
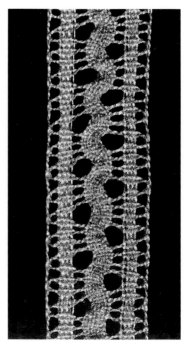

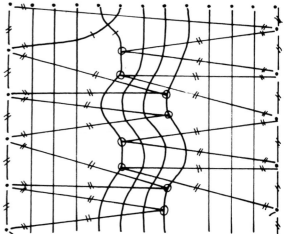

Meander-in-Braid 2

13 prs

Work 2 rows of cls.

† * W cls thro 2 prs, tw W once, cls and tw thro next pr, cls thro 4 prs, ts with next pr. Return thro 4 prs, tw W once, cls and tw thro next pr, cls thro 2 prs, tw W twice, edge st and pin. * W cls thro 2 prs, tw W once, cls and tw thro next pr, cls thro 4 prs, tw W and next pr once and make cls and tw with these 2 prs, W cls thro 2 prs, tw W twice, edge st and pin. (W is now on opposite side of work.)

Rpt from * to * once. †

Rpt from † to † for desired length, ending with half a repeat.

Care must be taken not to let this braid buckle or rise on the curves. If necessary, adjust the pinholes.

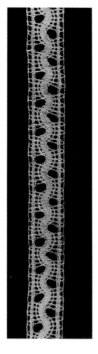
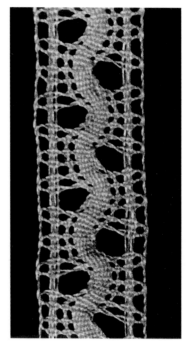

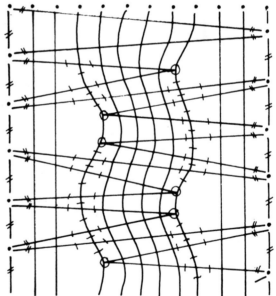

Mittens in Half Stitch

14 prs

Work ts with W and centre pr. Both these prs are now weavers.

Work lt W thro 5 prs to the lt in cls. Tw W twice, edge st and pin.

Work the same on other side with rt W.

* Work lt W thro 3 prs to rt in cls, tw W once, work W thro next 2 prs in hs, tw W once. Leave.

Work the same on the other side with rt W.

Two weavers in the centre: cls and tw twice.

Weavers have now changed sides.

Work lt W to the lt thro 2 prs in hs and thro 3 prs in cls, tw W twice, edge st and pin. Leave.

Work the same on other side with rt W. *

Rpt from * to * for desired length.

To discard one W when returning to ordinary braid: make ts in the centre with the two weavers. The W will be the pr on the side of the next pin hole to be worked. The remaining pr becomes a passive.

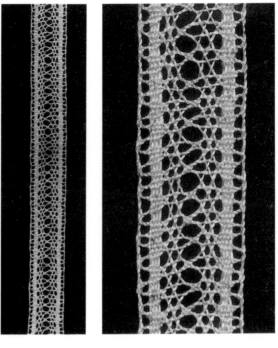

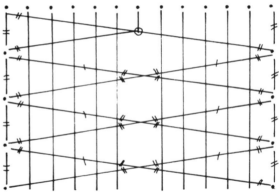

Ovals

14 prs

Ts with W and centre pr. Both these prs are weavers.

Lt W cls to lt thro 5 prs, tw W twice, edge st and pin. Leave.

Work rt W in similar manner.

† 2 centre prs: cls and tw.

* Lt W cls thro 4 prs, tw W once, cls and tw thro next pr. Leave.

Work rt W in similar manner.

2 centre prs (ie the two weavers) cls and tw.

Work lt centre pr to lt: cls and tw thro one pr, cls thro 4 prs, tw W twice, edge st and pin. Leave.

Work rt centre pr to rt in similar manner.

Rpt from * once more.

The whole pattern is then repeated from †.

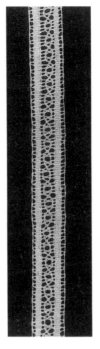
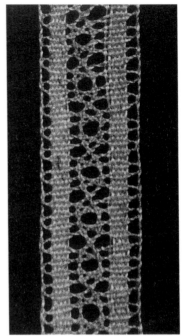

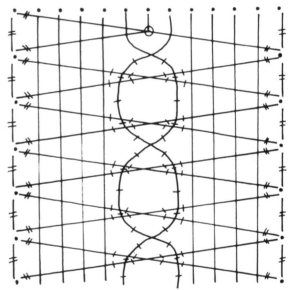

Pinwheel

14 prs

Ts with W and centre pr: the lt pr cls thro 1 pr to lt and the rt pr cls thro 1 pr to rt.

Two centre prs cls.

Tw twice 8 centre prs.

* Left side:
Take 6th pr from lt and work cls and 2 tw thro 2 prs to lt then cls thro 2 prs, tw W twice, edge st and pin. W cls thro 2 prs, tw W twice. Leave.

Take 7th pr from lt and work cls and 2 tw thro 3 prs to lt then cls thro 2 prs, tw W twice, edge st and pin. W cls thro 2 prs, tw W twice. Leave.

Right side:
Work in similar manner to lt side.

Centre 4 prs:
Lt 2 prs cross rt 2 prs in cls and 2 tw. Leave.

Centre of pinwheel is made as follows:

Left side:
Take 5th pr from lt and work cls and 2 tw thro 2 prs to rt. Leave. Take 4th pr from lt and work cls and 2 tw thro 2 prs to rt. Leave.

Right side:
Work in similar manner to lt side.

Then: 2 centre prs cls, the lt pr of these cls to lt thro 1 pr and the rt pr cls to rt thro 1 pr.

Two centre prs ts, the lt pr of these cls thro 1 pr to lt and the rt pr cls thro 1 pr to rt.

2 centre prs cls.

Tw twice 4 centre prs.

Rpt from * for desired length.

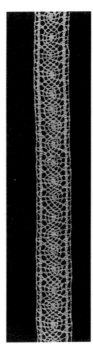

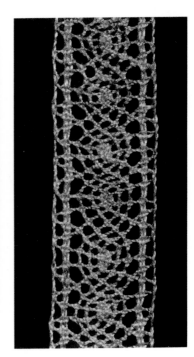

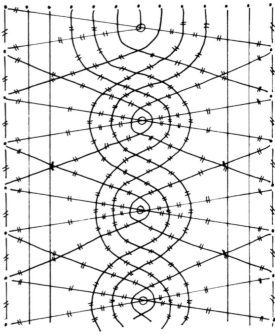

Ribbon

13 prs

Work 2 rows of cls.

† Cross centre 8 passive prs in groups of 2 prs with cls.

* Work W thro 1 pr, tw W twice, W continues to work across in cls but tw W once in the middle of each group of 2 prs and twice before the last passive, then tw W twice, edge st and pin. *

Centre 8 prs: tw once each.

Rpt from * to *. Leave W at edge. †

Rpt whole pattern from † to † for desired length, finishing with the crossing of the 8 prs.

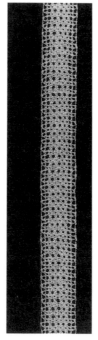
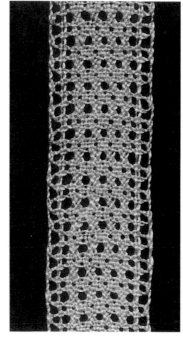

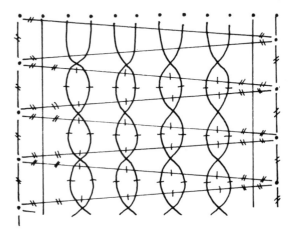

Spot Spider

14 prs

Work in cls braid.

Leave W at rt side, count back and make hs with 6th and 7th passive prs. Work the lt of these 2 prs thro 4 prs to the lt, tw W twice, edge st and pin. Leave.

Cls two centre prs

Left side:
Work W thro 4 prs to rt, tw last pr passed thro and work it back as new W thro 3 prs to lt, tw W twice, edge st and pin.

Work W thro 3 prs to rt. Leave.

Right side:
Work in similar manner to lt side.

Six centre prs:
Tw twice each pr.

Centre lt pr work thro 2 prs to lt in cls and tw.

Centre rt pr work thro 2 prs to rt in cls and tw.

Work spider with centre 4 prs. Tw each pr once.

Work 3rd pr from centre lt thro 2 prs to rt in cls and tw.

Work 3rd pr from centre rt thro 2 prs to lt in cls and tw.

Tw once more each 6 centre prs.

Note: a ts is made in the centre of the spider and no pin is used.

Cls two centre prs. Leave.

Right side:
Take 3rd pr from rt centre as W, work thro 3 prs to rt in cls, tw W twice, edge st and pin. Work W thro 4 prs to lt, tw last pr passed thro and work it back as new W thro 3 prs to rt, tw W twice, edge st and pin. Work W thro 4 prs to lt, tw W and next pr once and cross the 2 centre bobbins lt over rt (a reverse hs). Leave.

Left side:
Work in a similar manner to the rt side, but omit reverse hs.

Work W thro all prs and continue braid for desired length.

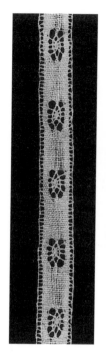
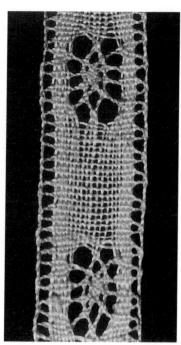
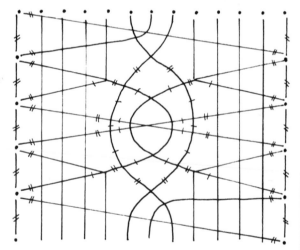

Star

14 prs

Ts with W and centre pr. Both these prs are now weavers and they work in cls throughout.

Work lt W to the lt thro 5 prs, tw W twice, edge st and pin. Leave.

Work rt W to the rt thro 5 prs, tw W twice, edge st and pin. Leave

Tw twice 2 centre prs, cls. Leave.

Left side:
* W thro 4 prs. Leave W and return with last pr passed thro as new W, thro 3 prs, tw W twice, edge st and pin.

W thro 3 prs, leave W and return with last pr passed thro as new W, thro 2 prs, tw W twice, edge st and pin. Leave.

Right side:
Work in similar manner to lt side.

Centre 6 prs:
Tw twice each pr.

Centre lt pr work in cls thro 2 prs to lt.

Centre rt pr work in cls thro 2 prs to rt.

Work spider with centre 4 prs (ts may be used for centre 2 prs).

Work outside lt pr thro 2 prs to rt.

Work outside rt pr thro 2 prs to lt.

Tw twice 6 centre prs.

Cross 2 centre prs in ws.

Left side:
W thro 3 prs. Leave W and return with last pr passed thro as new W, thro 2 prs, tw W twice, edge st and pin. Leave.

Right side:
Work in similar manner to lt side. *

Rpt from * to * for desired length.

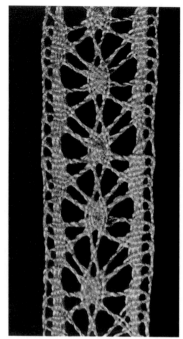

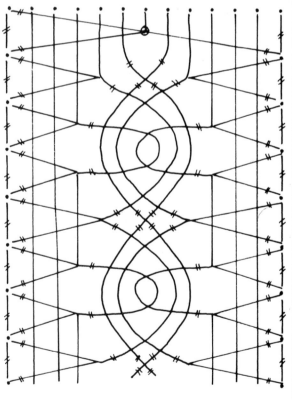

Trellis

14 prs

Ts with W and centre pr. Both these prs are now weavers. Work lt W to lt in cls thro 5 prs, tw W twice, edge st and pin. W thro one pr in cls. Leave. Work rt W to rt in similar manner.

* Divide centre 8 prs into two groups:

Lt group of 4 prs:
Cross lt 2 prs thro rt 2 prs in cls.

Tw all 4 prs twice.

Two lt prs both work out to lt edge, one at a time: the first (ie the lt) pr thro 2 prs in cls, tw twice, edge st and pin, return thro one pr. Leave. Then work the second pr thro 3 prs in cls, tw twice, edge st and pin, return thro one pr. Leave.

Rt group of 4 prs:
Work in similar manner to lt group.

Centre 4 prs: cross 2 lt prs thro 2 rt prs in cls.

Centre 8 prs: tw each pr twice. *

Rpt from * to * for desired length.

One twist instead of two may be used between the crossings for a less open effect.

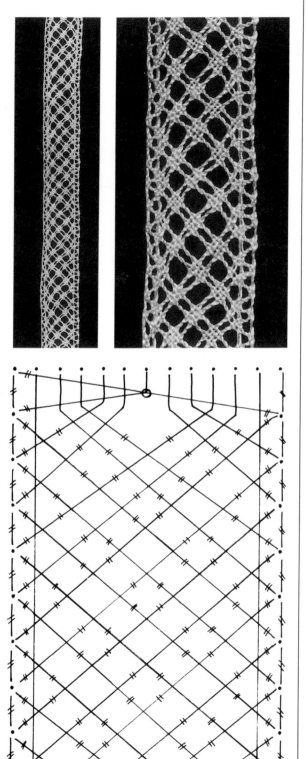

Zigzag Holes

14 prs

Left side:
* Work W thro 10 passive prs, leaving the last pr and edge pr. Work 1 cls with the last 2 prs passed thro, then work 1 cls with the rt pr and the W. Leave these 2 prs. Take the pr on the lt as the new W and work to the lt thro 8 prs, tw W twice, edge st and pin.

Rpt from * leaving out 2 more prs each time until 4 sets of 2 prs have been left out, leaving the W as the fourth pr from the lt.

Right side:
Take the 3rd pr from rt (ie the rt pr of the first set) as W and work to rt thro 1 pr, tw W twice, edge st and pin.

** Return thro 4 prs, take the last pr passed thro as new W and return thro 3 prs to rt, tw W twice, edge st and pin.

Rpt from ** adding 2 prs each time until three more sets have been taken in.

Zigzag holes:
Work the new W thro to the rt edge before commencing the same pattern in reverse on the opposite side.

Holes sloping in the same direction:
Any number of rows may be worked before recommencing the pattern. In the sample shown the pattern is continous.

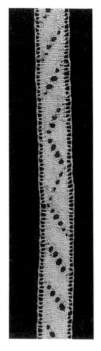
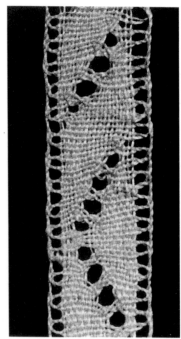
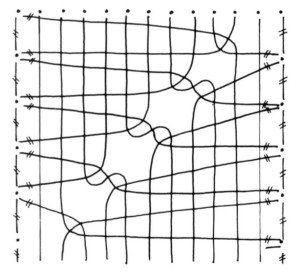

CHAPTER 4

Filling the Spaces

The spaces which occur between braids can be dealt with in a variety of ways, and are worked when the main part of the work is finished. The following notes describe some of the alternatives and how to work them. They can be worked in any direction and can fill any shape: the worker has complete freedom of choice in this.

Leaving the space empty

Not every space has to be filled. In some designs none are filled at all, the braids being joined only where they touch in passing. A few spaces left empty can alter the overall balance of a design to good effect, so careful consideration should always be given when deciding whether to leave a space empty or not.

Working a twisted bar

This works well within a long narrow shape. Sew in one pair. Twist this until it meets the required hole on the opposite side of the gap. Sew it into this hole, then twist it until it meets the required hole on the other side. When the pair is no longer required it is sewn out in the normal way.

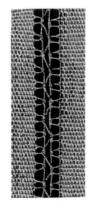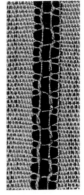

An alternative twisted bar

Sew in the pair. Twist it until it meets the required hole on the opposite side. Sew it in, then twist it, and carry it along the footside to another hole on the *same* side. Sew it in, then twist it and carry it back to the opposite side, and so on. There is more than one way of arranging this pair using this method and the reader is encouraged to experiment.

Working a plait

A plait can be used in the same way as a twisted bar.

To make a plait

Sew two pairs into the same hole. Work them together in half stitch, pulling up carefully after every two stitches, until the plait reaches the required hole on the opposite side. Keep the pairs as close to the pillow as possible while pulling up, and aim to keep the plait flat. When the plait is sewn into the edge take *both* threads of one pair through as one loop. Put both remaining threads through this loop, pull up and continue.

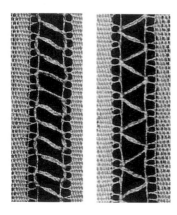

Working plaits with picots

Pinholes must be made where the picots are to fall.

To make a picot on the left

At the pinhole twist the weaver five times. Before the pin is put in it must be twisted round the left thread of this pair. To do this, hold the bobbin in the left hand. Take the pin in the right. Lay the pin on top of the thread, then direct the point down, under the thread and towards yourself, then back over the thread and into the hole. Do not let the bobbin drop as this loop must be kept slack for the time being. Take the other thread of the pair in a clockwise direction round the pin, then pull the two threads up at the same time. They should twist together and lock round the pin. The plait can then be continued.

To make a picot on the right

This time the pin is twisted round the thread on the right side of the pair. Take the pin *under* the thread first, then back over the thread and towards yourself, and down into the pinhole. The second thread is then carried round the pin in an anticlockwise direction before the two threads are pulled up together.

When two picots are made facing one another across a plait, make the first picot as above (either to the left or right). Work a cloth stitch with both pairs and then go on to make the second picot.

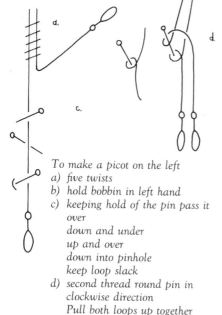

To make a picot on the left
a) *five twists*
b) *hold bobbin in left hand*
c) *keeping hold of the pin pass it*
   over
   down and under
   up and over
   down into pinhole
   keep loop slack
d) *second thread round pin in*
   clockwise direction
   Pull both loops up together

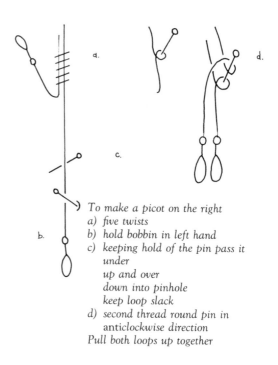

To make a picot on the right
a) *five twists*
b) *hold bobbin in left hand*
c) *keeping hold of the pin pass it*
   under
   up and over
   down into pinhole
   keep loop slack
d) *second thread round pin in*
   anticlockwise direction
   Pull both loops up together

Another arrangement of picots and plaits

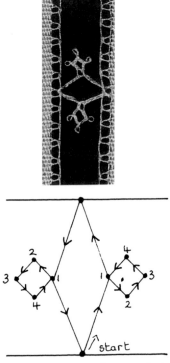

Sew in two pairs and plait as far as pinhole 1. There is no picot here, instead both pairs are given an extra twist and the pin put between them before the plait is continued to pinhole 2. Make a picot at this pinhole. The plait is continued round the diamond shape with picots being made at each pinhole. When the plait gets back to pinhole 1, remove the pin and sew the plait into this loop. Replace the pin and take the plait to the braid and sew it into the edge. Return with it to the opposite side, working the second diamond shape on the way. Sew the pairs off into the hole into which they were first sewn.

When this arrangement of picots appears on an outside edge (see photograph on page 117) proceed in the same way, using the edge pair and the weaver pair to make the plait. Link both parts of the plait together before taking the weaver back into the work.

Using two pairs to fill a gap

One pair is sewn in on each side of the gap. The two pairs are crossed in the middle and taken out to the opposite edge, where they are sewn in before returning to cross again. They can be crossed in a variety of ways.

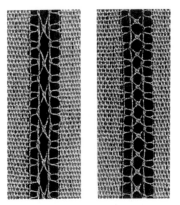

Using four pairs to fill a gap

This can look very similar to a braid. The four pairs can be crossed in a variety of ways, two of which are shown here, but do experiment with these yourself.

Variation one. Sew two pairs into each side. Twist each pair three times. Make a spider with these four pairs using a turning stitch at the centre instead of a pin. Twist the legs three times each. Take the outside leg (on both sides) to the edge and sew it in. Twist it three times and leave. Now take the inside leg (on both sides) through the sewn-in pair in cloth stitch. Twist it three times and sew it into the edge. Twist all four pairs three times and bring them back to the centre to work the next spider.

Variation two. This is worked in the same way, except that the pairs are twisted twice, and pass through one another in cloth stitch at the centre, (as in the first half of a spider).

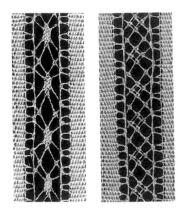

Using another braid

Where the shape and size of a space is suitable, another braid can be used to fill the gap. This is worked as a braid but without footings, the weavers being sewn into the adjoining braid on both sides. The width of the braid can be adjusted by altering the number of straight passives. Some braids are worked using multiples of two/three/ four pairs. These can be adjusted by adding or subtracting pairs in those multiples. If the work is very wide, use support pins. (See page 147.)

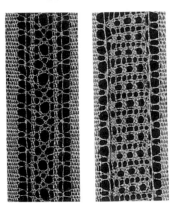

Using an unpricked filling

This method is useful for those tiny spaces which need a filling but are either too small or too awkward a shape to be pricked in the ordinary way. Because they are not pricked the stitches can be opened out, or pulled closer together when the shape makes it necessary. Two examples are shown here and other stitches and grounds can be adapted.

Trolley Net

Sew the pairs in, in sets of two. Join the pairs at each crossing with x t t t. Sew pairs at the end of the row into the braid and bring back into the work where necessary. It is best, but not essential, to work diagonally. Sew in new pairs as required.

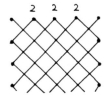

Mechlin Net

Sew pairs in, in sets of two. Make plaits (four half stitches) with two pairs from opposite sets. (See diagram.) At the end of each plait twist each pair twice more. Sew the pairs at either end of the row into the edge of the adjoining braid. Work the remaining pairs together in plaits, taking one pair from each of the previous plaits. Give each pair an extra two twists at the end of the plait. No pairs are sewn into the edge this time. Work the next row of plaits, this time using the pairs which were sewn into the edge and left. Continue in this way until the space is filled. Sew in extra pairs as needed.

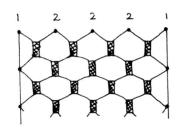

Using a pricked ground or filling stitch

These can be worked to fill any shape and in any direction. Some look the same whichever way they are worked whilst others have a definite 'grain'. Consider your design carefully in order to achieve the effect you intend, especially if several neighbouring shapes are to be worked with the same stitch. Prick according to the instructions in Chapter Seven. If possible, turn the pillow and work *across* the narrowest part. This will take fewer pairs.

Pairs are sewn in and out as required. If pairs are needed again soon there is no need to cut them off. Carry them along the edge of the work and sew them in again in their new position.

Many of the ground and filling stitches are pricked to the same basic dot pattern. Though the spacing between the dots may differ from stitch to stitch, the stitches usually adapt well to a universal pricking. This means that a pricking can be put in before work is begun, but the decision about the actual stitch to be used, made later. Use different sizes of graph paper to plot the spacing which suits you.

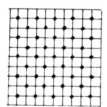

The Book of Bobbin Lace Stitches, by Bridget M. Cook and Geraldine Stott, published by Batsford, is an invaluable source of reference for stitches to use in this manner. Three examples are shown here. (Instructions for working other fillings are included with the worknotes accompanying each pricking.)

Valenciennes

Sew pairs in, in sets of four. (See diagram.) Plaits are made with four half stitches. Joins are made by half stitch, pin, half stitch. Note that only one pair from each plait (the inside pair) is used at this join. After the join has been worked it unites with the outside pair and continues in the plait. When there is an odd pair at the end of a row, sew it into the edge and bring it back to make a plait in the following row. Sew in extra pairs as needed.

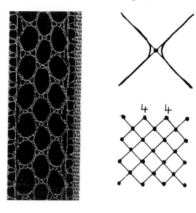

Cobwebs

Sew pairs in, in sets of two. Twist all pairs three times. * Taking pairs as indicated in the diagram, cross each set with half stitch. Place a pin between these pairs but do not close. A new pair is sewn into the edge. It works through all the sets in cloth stitch, and is twisted three times between each set before being sewn into the opposite edge. Work half stitch with each set of two pairs and twist each pair twice more. Repeat from * but instead of sewing in a new pair, carry the pair which works horizontally, along the edge to its new position.

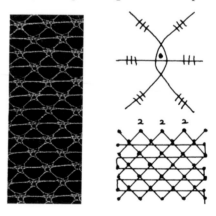

Cane Ground

All joins are worked with cloth stitch and twist (x t x t). For the order of working the pairs, see the diagram.

 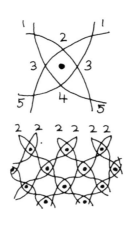

Using spiders and fish

These appear in a number of fillings (and braids) and lend themselves to improvisation. Braids using spiders and fish are easily adapted for use as fillings. Instructions for working a basic spider and a basic fish are given in Chapter Eight. Experiment with them yourself.

Note: Borrowing ideas from other sources is another way of filling the spaces, for example, the purl picots and ten stick used in Honiton lace are suitable and instructions for these are given in Chapter Eight. Finally filling the gaps is a wonderful way of being inventive so do experiment yourself with different fillings and ideas.

CHAPTER 5

Traditional Patterns

In this chapter the designs have been based on, and adapted from, the traditional floral shapes seen in old lace, mainly Milanese and Flemish. The pattern notes give the names of the braids used in the lace shown in the photographs, but the worker should feel free to make substitutions. The first pattern is for beginners, or those experimenting with decorated braids for the first time. At the end of the chapter there are four motifs without instruction: these are for the worker to interpret.

A beginner's piece

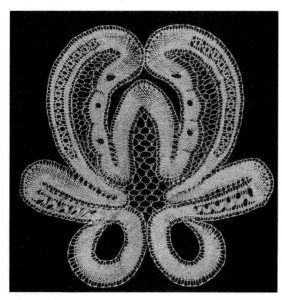

It is recommended that small samples of the Meander-in-braid 1, Ovals and Hole 1 should be worked. It may also be helpful to read the notes on sewings, blind pins and the scroll method before commencing work. For the abbreviations see page 24.

Thread: Copley Marshall No. 80
12 prs
The cls braid is worked with an edge pr on each side, the edge pr and W should be twisted twice and the pin put up under two pairs.

Commence at the point of the ring

Set a pin in hole A and hang four prs open round it. Work cls with the 2 lt prs and tw all four prs twice each. The outside 2 prs are edge prs and the inside 2 prs are passives. Set up a temporary pin at hole B inside the rt edge pr. Hang 2 prs open on this, take the lt of the 2 prs as W and work to the lt thro 2 passive prs, make edge st and pin in hole C. Work W to rt thro 2 passive prs and the pr hanging on the temporary pin, make edge st, remove temporary pin and replace under edge pr and W. Continue in cls braid, laying in one new pr in each row (see page 144) until 12 prs are in use, at the same time making a blind pin (backstitch) on every pin on the inside of the curve.

When the braid circle reaches the starting point, the W should be sewn in to connect the work. Pull up carefully, continue the braid and make two more sewings in the next two holes on that side of the work. In the next row, with the W on the rt, commence Meander-in-braid 1 (see page 48). As there are only 12 prs in use, the opening half stitch is made with the 6th and 7th passive prs, and there are only 2 prs of passives each side of the Meander instead of 3 prs.

Continue the Meander until one hole remains on the lt. The last Meander should be on the rt. The lt W becomes a passive again by working it in a reverse half-stitch with the lt pr from the Meander.

Continue in cls braid using the rt W. Work the last hole on the lt, tw the edge pr once and it now becomes a passive pr. Use the scroll method (see page 20) to work round the curve. When the rt and lt holes are level, continue with the braid and take one sewing with the W into each pinhole of the previous work on the lt. When pinhole X is reached, put the edge pr aside, to be used again when the braid returns. Continue braid until the next four pinholes on the rt have been worked and at these holes tw W twice and pin under the W (no edge st). At this point the braid will be narrowing considerably and one pr can be left hanging at each of the remaining holes on the rt, the last hole being using as a pivot or swing pin.

When the last sewing has been made on the lt, the end passive pr is twisted twice and again becomes the edge pr. After the pivot pin has been used enough times to bring the pinholes level, the prs left hanging can be brought back into the braid one at a time, as follows:

> Work W from the lt edge through all the passive prs and through one hanging pr, which should not be twisted. Tie this pr once and use as the

new W leaving the old W as passives. At the remaining pinholes where no pairs are hanging, it is necessary to sew in the W. At the appropriate hole take up the edge pr on the rt, which has been put aside.

Work one row of cls before commencing Ovals (see page 51). There will be only three passive prs on either side of the Ovals. It will be necessary to make a few blind pins (backstitch) as the work continues round the curve. The last Oval should be made when four pinholes remain to be worked on the lt. Continue in cls braid and when the last pinhole on the lt is reached, start the scroll method to turn the curve.

Continue in cls braid and work a hole (see Hole 1, page 40) in the centre of each scallop. A division can be made between the scallops by twisting the lt five passive prs three times each.

When six pinholes remain on the rt, put aside the rt edge pr, to be used again when the braid returns. At these remaining six holes, tw W twice and pin under the W. When the sixth hole is reached start the scroll method to work round the curve. At the same time, sew the W into the braid on the lt, where the pinholes are close to the previously made work.

When the scroll is complete and the holes level, continue in cls braid, taking up the edge pr which has been put aside, and making blind pins to keep the work level, until the next curve is reached. Again use the scroll method.

Complete the second half of the motif to match the first, remembering when working the Meander-in-braid in the second half to tie out the lt edge pr and sew it in again after the last sewing has been made on the lt.

When finishing off as the braid narrows to the point, throw out one pr in each of the last six rows and sew off and tie the remaining pairs into the pinholes of the braid. Cut off all the pairs closely.

Centre filling: 6 prs

Mechlin net
To begin, each pr should be twisted twice, then hs pin between, hs three times, tw both prs once more.

Commence by sewing in one pr each side and slightly above the top hole. Work the first hole. Sew in two more prs, one on the lt and one on the rt, and slightly above the next two holes to be worked. * Work the lt hole with the two lt prs and the lt pr is then sewn into the braid. Work the rt side in similar manner. Then work the next hole with the two centre pairs. Rpt from * until the filling widens, when it will be necessary to sew in two more pairs, one on the lt and one on the rt. Complete the filling, sew and tie off each pr into the braid. Cut off all the pairs closely.

Side fillings: 3 prs

Trolley net (or Bucks Point Ground)
No pins are necessary to support the net. Commence by sewing in two prs, one each side of the top point. Tw each pr three times.

The net: hs and tw each pr twice more.

Sew the prs into each side of the braid and sew the third pr into the next hole on the outside of the curve. Work in diagonal rows from the outside of the curve to the inside. There should be one sewing in each hole on the outside curve, but it will be necessary occasionally to sew into the bars between the pinholes on the inside of the curve to keep the filling level.

To finish sew in and tie off each pair at the bottom point, and cut them off closely.

Lily

Designed and worked by Jane Read.
Thread: Copley Marshall No. 80

The braid is continuous throughout, commencing in the centre, at the base of one petal, with a false footing. The number of pairs increased as the braid widens.

Braids: Trellis
         Hole 1
         Pinwheel – variation
         Figure-of-Eight 1
         Beads
         Basketweave

Note: In the pinwheel variation the set of twists nearest the centre (on weavers and passives) were omitted.

Flower

Based on a traditional design and worked by Eileen Mills.
Thread: Retors d'Alsace No. 50

Trace on the pattern the path of the braids which are in three main sections.

ORDER OF WORKING

1. Commence with the scroll at the base of the flower, at the pinhole marked with a ring. As the work narrows on the final scallop pairs may be thrown out. The remaining pairs should be tied back before being cut off.
2. Make the scroll at the base of the leaf and sew off into the first scroll.
3. Fill in the braid from the tip of the leaf down to the base of the flower, throwing out pairs as the braid narrows, finally sewing off into the second braid.
4. Make the third scroll, sewing off between the two braids.

Braids: Hole 1
          Cloth Divisions 1 and 3
          Ovals
          Maltese Spot

Fillings: Spiders
          Trolley net using only two pairs
          Apple Blossom

Apple Blossom

All joins x t x. Plaits before and after each blossom. Picots at pins 1, 2, 3, 4.

Note: The braids were connected with top sewings which shows to good effect on this piece.

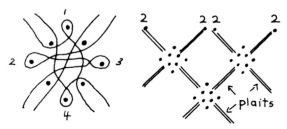

Flower Spray

Based on a traditional design and worked by Kathleen Gidden.
Thread: Retors d'Alsace No. 60

The braids are made in seven sections. By tracing the path of the braids it is possible to work out which sections should be made first so that other sections can be sewn in. (See page 17.)

Picots have been worked on the petals but not on the leaves.

ORDER OF WORKING
1. Work the centre ring and one petal.
2. Work the lower petal.
3. Work the remaining three petals.
4. Work the two leaves.

Braids: Hole 1
            Cloth Divisions 3
            Zigzag Holes
            Buds – 6-Pin
            Maltese Spot
            Lazy-Tongs

Fillings: Cobweb
            Fishes
            Spiders
            Haloed Spider

Haloed Spider

All joins x t x. Twists as indicated on diagram.

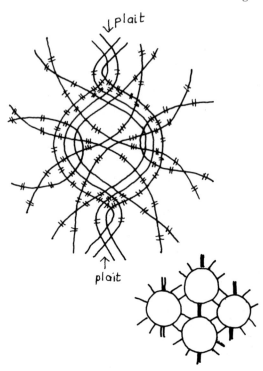

Tie Ends

Based on a traditional design and worked by Hazel Goatham.
Thread: Brok No. 100

If picots are to be made, a second row of holes should be pricked on the outside edge of the pattern, taking care to leave a plain edge which can be applied to material. (See page 147).

ORDER OF WORKING
1. Work the first braid begining with the scroll.
2. Work the second braid. Sew pairs in at the braid's wider end, then pairs can be thrown out as the work narrows, leaving only a few pairs to be sewn off.
3. Work the fillings

Braids: Horseshoes
       Hole 1
       Cloth Divisions 1

Filling: Daisy Spider

Daisy Spider

All joins x t x. Extra twist round pin 'a'. Twist legs three times.

Note: The worker has used a variation of Cloth Divisions, twisting some of the passive pairs and working the weavers through the twisted pairs in cloth stitch and twist.

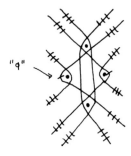
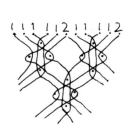

Tabs for Revers or Collar

Designed by Patricia Read and worked by Hazel Goatham.
Thread: Brok No. 100

If it is decided to work cane ground for a filling, as in the sample, the pinholes for this should be pricked before setting up. If picots are to be worked, these too should be pricked on the outside edge of the pattern, leaving a plain edge where the work will be mounted onto material. The braid is in two sections, the main one of which should be worked first. The small section, which consists of three scallops, can then be sewn into the main braid.

Braids: Cloth Stitch
         Half Stitch
         Cloth Divisions 2
         Hole 1
         Spot Spider
         Ovals

Filling: Cane Ground

Cane Ground

All joins x t x t
See diagram for order of working.

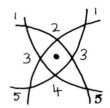

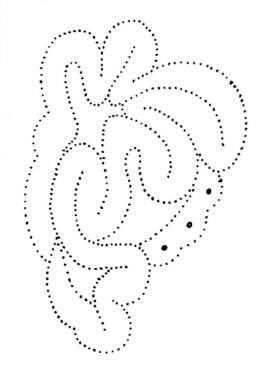

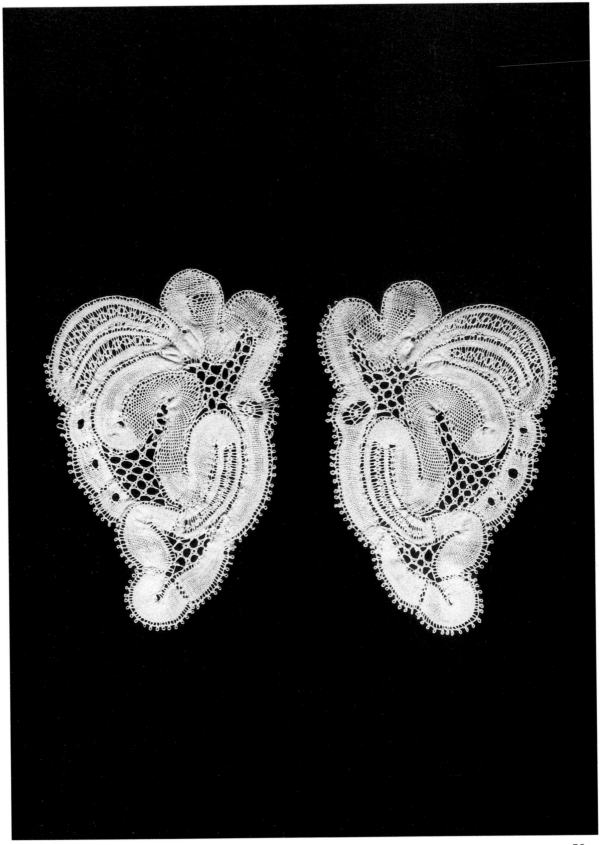

Square Mat

Designed and worked by Jane Read.
Thread: Copley Marshall No. 80

This is shown as a mat, but one quarter of the design could be used as a handkerchief corner. The braid is continuous and commences at the point mid-way along one side.

Braids: Meander-in-Braid 1
        Holes – 1
        Figure-of-Eight 3
        Buds – 6-pin
        Spot Spider
        Small Plaits

The small plaits have been used at the mid-way points between the corners. Note that they have also been used on some of the curves – a way of enabling the worker to turn a sharp bend without the use of the scroll or other methods. The two pairs of each plait are left out as the braid is worked to the tip of the curve and then taken in again when the work is turned.

Leaves

Leaves

Designed and worked by Patricia Read.
Thread: Copley Marshall No. 80

The design is based on a leaf shape in an old Flemish flounce (see *The History of Lace* by Margaret Simeon, page 56). The scalloped edge on the inside of the work is a feature often found in both Flemish and Milanese braid work. The simple trolley net seems to show up the scallop effect better than a more fancy filling. If picots are to be worked, a second row of holes should be pricked on the outside edge of the pattern. (See page 147.) Trace the pattern to see how much braid can be worked continuously.

ORDER OF WORKING

1. Work the short stem first. This forms the key into which most of the other braids can be connected. Begin at the top with false picots or false footing. Fourteen small tallies are worked down the centre of the braid, using two passive pairs between two rows of cloth stitch. Reduce the number of pairs as the braid narrows and tie back the remaining bobbins at the end.

2. The outlines of all the leaves can be worked next. The bobbins should be tied back at the end of the leaf which has a small stem at the end.
3. Work the inner braids.
4. Work the fillings.

Braids: Hole 2
              Cloth Divisions 1
              Buds – 6-pin
              Zigzag Holes
              Archway
              Figure-of-Eight 1

Fillings: Trolley Net
              Fishes with Two Horizontals
              Toile Star

Toile Star

All pairs entering and leaving have three twists. All pairs crossed in cloth stitch.

Braid Sampler

Designed and worked by Jane Read.
Thread: Copley Marshall No. 80

The symmetry of this pattern makes a simple yet
striking piece of lace. The fact that no fillings have
been used gives a clean-cut appearance to the work
and it can be compared with early Milanese work,
for example the panel of seventeenth century
Milanese bobbin lace displayed at the Victoria &
Albert Museum, London. The braid is continuous
throughout and commences across the braid at the
ringed holes close to the centre.

Braids: Crescent
        Horseshoes
        Archway
        Meander-in-Braid 1
        Pinwheel – variation
        Beads
        Kisses

Note: In the Pinwheel variation the set of twists
nearest the centre (on weavers and passives) were
omitted.

One half of the pattern is given on page 82.

The arrows indicate the half-way line.

Braid Sampler

Oval

Oval

Designed by Jane Read and worked by Sheila Watler.
Thread: D.M.C. Retors d'Alsace No. 60

One half of the pattern is given. For a small mat, the two narrow scrolls on either side can be omitted.

ORDER OF WORKING
1. Begin with the scroll at the head of the large flower shape. This braid also ends in a scroll and another small braid works into it.
2. Work the other side to match.
3. Work the two narrow scrolls.
4. Work all the fillings.

This completes the first half which should be removed from the pattern. The second half can then be made on the same pricking. When the two narrow scrolls are made they can be joined with sewings to the two scrolls on the first half.

Braids: Figure-of-Eight 1
          Maltese Spot
          Cloth Divisions 1

Fillings: Fishes with Four Horizontals
          Half Stitch

Collar

Designed by Patricia Read and worked by Victoria Saunders
Thread: D.M.C. Retors d'Alsace No. 60

When worn, this gives a V-shape neckline. It is recommended that a tissue paper template should be cut from the outline of the collar pattern and fitted to check for size and shape. It should not be difficult to re-draw and re-dot the design, or part of it, to obtain a pattern which will fit the wearer.

ORDER OF WORKING
1. Begin where five holes have been circled. This braid is the major part of the work.
2. Fill in the short length of braid which begins close to the original starting point.
3. Make the next adjoining braid.
4. Work the other half of the collar.
5. Work the back inset – a flower shape which is attached to both sides of the collar.
6. Work all the fillings.
7. Work the neck band, starting and finishing with a scroll. (See page 20.)

The fillings should be worked in the first half of the collar, if it is intended to remove this piece from the pillow before the second half is made.

Braids: Basketweave
Cloth Divisions 1
Holes 1
Beads
Maltese Spot
Archway
May Bud
Meander-in-Braid 2
Horsehoes
Mittens in Half Stitch

Fillings: Mechlin Net
Cobwebs
Trolley net
Spiders

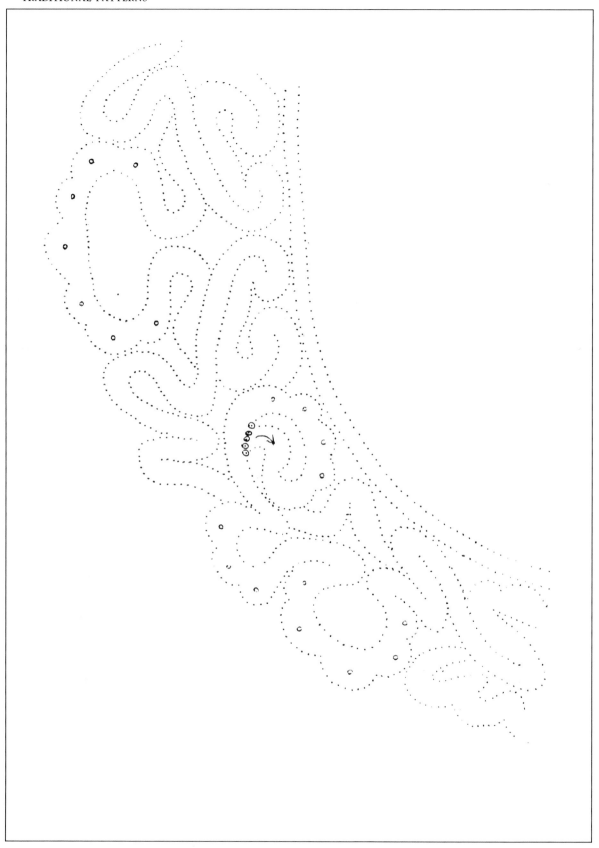

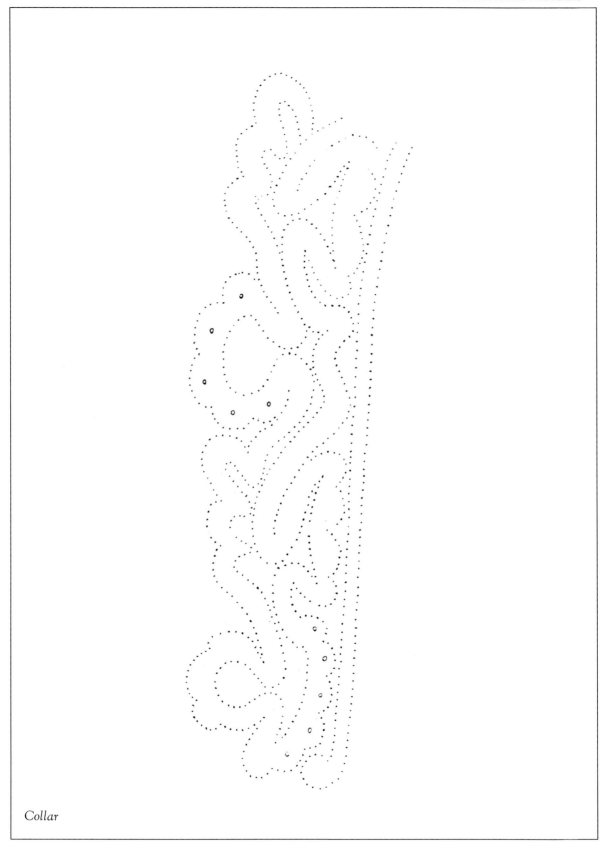

Collar

Collar

Collar

Designed and worked by Patricia Read.
Thread: Copley Marshall 80

Each motif is complete in itself. These may be joined together on the pillow as the work progresses. The pattern should be reversed for the second side of the collar. The picots are optional but if they are to be worked, a second row of holes should be added to the outside edge of the pattern. (See page 147.)

ORDER OF WORKING

1. Begin with the first motif of the leaves. The curved leaf-shape begins with a scroll at the end of the collar. (See page 20.) To start the smaller leaf shape, pairs can be sewn into the larger leaf. Lastly, work the small scroll.
2. Work the second motif of the flower. Begin and end with a scroll. Work the small pieces of connecting braid.
3. The next leaf shape should be worked in a similar manner to the first.
4. Work the third motif of the flower beginning and ending at one of the inner curves of the braid.
5. The motif at the centre back of the collar is a larger version of the second motif and should be worked in a similar manner.
6. The remaining four motifs are made in reverse order to correspond with the first side of the collar.
7. Work the neck-edge braid. This should be connected to all the motifs as it is worked.

Braids: Cloth Divisions 1
         Cloth Divisions 2
         Zigzag Holes
         Figure-of-Eight 1
         Half Stitch with plaited divisions
         Hole 1
         Beads

Fillings: Figure-of-Eight 3
          Valenciennes ground
          Haloed Fish
          Spiders
          Italian Fish
          Toile Star variation

Toile Star variation

All pairs entering and leaving, twist twice.
All pairs crossed in cloth stitch.

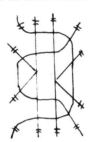

Collar

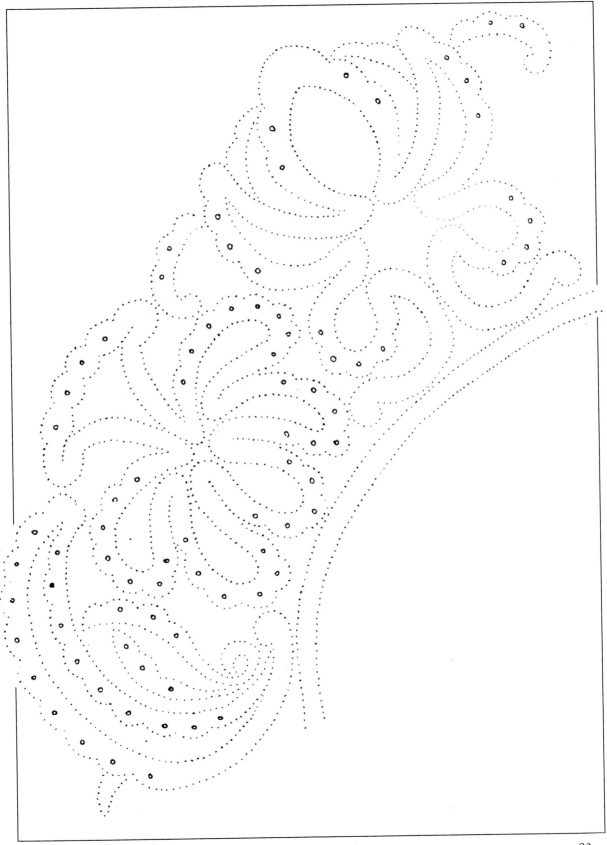

Oval

Based on a traditional design and worked by
Jennifer Hanney.
Thread: Mettler No. 60

One quarter of the pattern is given which should
be traced or photocopied on tracing paper, turned
over and joined where the arrow is marked. This
will then give half the pattern. The braid is in three
sections. The main one is continuous right round
the mat and the other two border the narrow sides.

ORDER OF WORKING

1. Commence at the holes which are circled.
   Continue this braid to the end of the pricking.
   Leave these bobbins aside.
2. Sew in pairs for the second braid on the same
   side as the bobbins which have been left.
   When this second braid has also reached the
   end of the pricking, leave both sets of bobbins
   together.
3. Work all the fillings.
4. Support the bobbins which are hanging from
   the braids. Remove the pins, turn the pillow
   round and re-pin the short double braid to the
   other side of the pricking. Also re-pin the
   narrow strip of braid where the work
   commenced.
5. Complete the first (inner) braid.
6. The second braid can then be finished and
   sewn off into the first braid.
7. Work the third braid, to match the second, to
   the end of the pricking. Leave the bobbins
   aside.
8. Work all the fillings.
9. Support the remaining bobbins whilst, once
   again, removing the pins, turning the pillow
   and repinning the small amount of braid
   necessary for the completion of the third and
   last braid.
10. Work the last two fillings.

Braids: Archway
         Cloth Divisions 1
         Maltese Spot
         Buds – 4-Pin
         Horseshoes
         Star
         Spot Spider
         Trellis
         Fishes with Four Horizontals

Fillings: Cobweb
           Mechlin Net
           Fishes with Two Horizontals
           Fishes with Four Horizontals
           Trolley Net

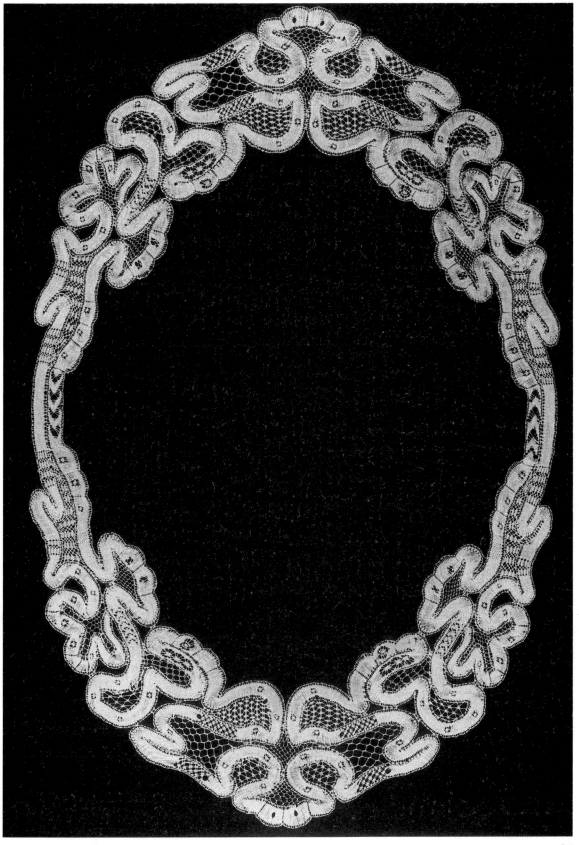

Oval

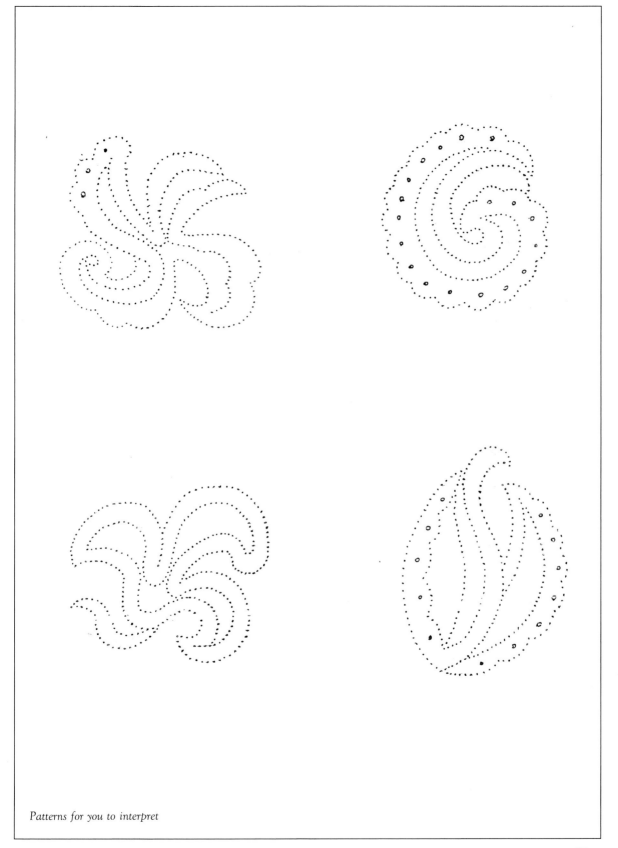

Patterns for you to interpret

CHAPTER 6

A Modern Approach

Experimentation

The attraction of making this kind of lace is that no two prickings need ever be worked in the same way. That means you can work your own version of any pricking in this book. Doing this successfully depends on an attitude of mind, rather than on having a vast array of techniques at your command. Do not be discouraged because you feel you have not been making lace long enough to experiment on your own. Apart from the basic techniques, which are fully explained in Chapters Two, Three and Four, all you need is a willingness to think for yourself and the patience to try again when an idea does not work.

When working traditional lace you *must* observe certain rules. Each pair of bobbins has its appointed place. In braid lace, not only are there fewer pairs to manipulate, but those pairs do not have to be left in a particular place, in order to work the next part of the pattern. This makes it easier to experiment and to find your own way of doing things. Only one part of the work, the particular braid being worked at that moment, is affected by what you do. If an experiment goes hopelessly wrong, only that one part need be cut out. What has gone before remains untouched.

Nor is it necessary to think out experimental changes in advance. Ideas will present themselves to you as you work. If an idea does occur, then try it out. If it does not turn out the way you expected it to, it is easy enough to back pedal a few rows. One does not hesitate to go into reverse when one makes a mistake with a stitch, so why should going into reverse with an idea be any different? Listen to what your subconscious tells you. It knows as much about lace making as you do. Maybe you know more than you are aware of.

Having already discovered how easily the threads can be manipulated when working the decorated braids, try manipulating the threads in order to put your own ideas into practice. Start in a small way, putting in or taking out a twist then, as you gain in confidence, experiment more. With practice you will find the ideas flow freely.

The working of a pattern can be as simple, or as complex, as you choose to make it. Consider how one deals with a basic recipe in the kitchen changing it to suit one's own tastes and requirements, but staying within one's own capabilities as a cook. Look upon each pricking as a basic recipe: it is there for you to experiment with in any way you wish.

The aim of this chapter is *not* to give you detailed instructions for working the prickings as they appear in the photographs. (Though you can copy them exactly if you so wish.) If you follow the basic instructions as presented in Chapters Two, Three and Four, you will have all the information you need to work on your own. Remember, each braid has its own beginning and its own end. Each one is finished before the next one is started. The aim of this chapter is to further your understanding of the way in which the patterns are put together. Once you understand how this is done a whole new sphere of lace making opens up. You are then ready to go a stage further and design your own patterns. This will be explained in greater detail in Chapter Seven.

Having decided to work your own version of a pricking does not mean you cannot learn by looking at what other lace makers have done, in fact some would say it is the *only* way you can learn. So compare prickings and photographs, observe which decorated braids are used, and whether you consider them effective; note how the same braid can create different effects and how the braids have been joined. Decide the order in which they were worked (the notes accompanying the prickings will help here). Trace off the prickings, with a line instead of dots. This has the same effect as writing down figures when you are trying to add them up: your awareness is intensified. Observe how different workers have tackled similar problems in different ways and consider how you would have tackled the problem. Your ideas are just as valid as any other lacemaker's. They could be better.

All decorated braids are interchangeable of course, but it is worth experimenting with these too. Just a slight variation in the manner of working can change a braid very effectively. There are two good examples of this on page 134, the back of the fish being a variation of Archway and the waves a variation of Ribbon. Try making up your own braids. Because braids are worked with such few pairs, stitches can be manipulated in a way that would be impossible without pins elsewhere, so do experiment!

If you want to work a particular pattern but do not like the spacing of the dots, change them. Make a tracing of the pattern, using a line instead of dots, and re-dot it, according to the instructions in Chapter Seven. Be prepared, as work proceeds, to prick extra holes, or to leave holes unworked if you consider it necessary. The pinholes are there to help you, not dictate to you.

Do not worry about which thread to use. As long as the thickness of the thread and the scale of the pricking are compatible, it does not matter. Work a short length of plain braid in the thread of your choice and you will see immediately whether it suits the pricking. Remember, just as you can change a thread to suit a pricking, so you can enlarge, or reduce, a pricking to match a particular thread. There is nothing to stop you using string, if you really want to, as long as it matches the pricking.

Are you still hesitating? Be bold! You could surprise yourself. All the patterns in this chapter have been worked according to the basic principles set out earlier in the book, but in addition every worker has added something extra in the way the braids have all been put together and decorated. You could say they have put their signatures on their work. You can do the same.

How to Begin.

1. Choose your pattern.
2. Read Chapter Two and Chapter Four carefully.
3. Trace your pattern so that you understand how the pieces fit together.
4. Decide which is the key braid.
5. Look at Chapter Three and decide which braids *you* are going to use.
6. Take a deep breath, and begin. And like Topsy, your lace will just grow.

Palm Tree

An original design worked by Joy Wood.
Thread: Copley Marshall No. 80

ORDER OF WORKING
1. *Main foliage of tree:* Worked as a continuous braid.
2. *Top knot of foliage:* Notice how the pairs have been carried across from one side to the other.
3. *Foliage at base of tree:* Starting from either end.
4. *Trunk:* In any order or direction.
5. *The shadow/water:* Notice how the worker has deviated from the pricking and worked another braid here.

Braids: Meander-in-Braid 1
       Basketweave
       Cloth Divisions
       Figure-of-Eight 3
       Beads
       Maltese Spot

Woman with Parasol

An original design worked by Lucy Kincaid.
Thread: Retors d'Alsace No. 50

ORDER OF WORKING

1. *Waistband:* Start and finish with a false footing.
2. *Bodice:* a) The sides, from shoulder to waistband. Start with a false footing. b) The centre, from neck to waistband.
3. *Sleeves:* From cuff to shoulder. Start with a false footing.
4. *Hands:* From finger tips to wrists. Twists for finger divisions.
5. *Bonnet band:* From top to bottom. Start with a false footing. Pairs carried from the band into the back of the bonnet, which is worked from the bottom upwards. Finish with a false footing. Final four pairs sewn into band.
6. *Bonnet brim:* From top to bottom. Start and finish with a false footing. Final four pairs sewn off into band.
7. *Neck:* In any direction.
8. *Skirt:* Each panel from hem towards waistband.
9. *Shoe:* Worked from the sole upwards. Start with a false footing.
10. *Parasol:* The main section from top to bottom. Pairs carry on to make spike at bottom.
11. *Parasol handle:* Note that this was pinned under one pair at the edge.

Braids: Archway
A variation on Archway, worked with fewer pairs, resulting in six legs instead of eight
Cloth with twists
Basketweave
Mittens in Half Stitch

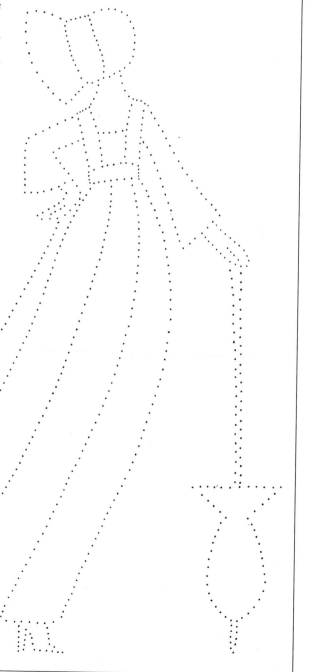

Phoenix

A design based on a Chinese paper cut and worked by Peggy Jones.
Thread: Tannen No. 80

ORDER OF WORKING
1. *Head:* From the top of the head to the tip of the crest feather. (See diagram.)
2. Finish the head.
3. *Feathers:* Start from the tips and work towards body. See diagram for order of working.
4. *Body:* Sew into wing to start.
5. Braid leading from the 'chin' of the bird to the flower.
6. Finish flower. (Purl picots on outside.)
7. The lower frond, then its leaf.
8. All remaining sections.

Braids: Basketweave
Holes 1
Beads
Cloth Divisions – 3
Half Stitch
Cloth Stitch and Twist
Maltese Spot

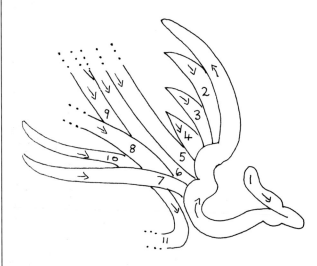

Work braids in this order

See pricking page 106

104

Phoenix

Madonna

Madonna

A design based on a Christmas card and worked by
Kathleen Gidden.
Thread: Copley Marshall 80.

ORDER OF WORKING

1. *Robe:* Cloth stitch braids from top of Madonna's head, to top of Child's head. Small braid round Child's face.
2. Half stitch filling between braids on robe.
3. *Madonna's hair.*
4. *Madonna's face:* From chin to hairline.
5. *Child's face.*
6. Space between Child's head and halo.
7. Outer ring of Madonna's halo.
8. The inner ring of Madonna's halo. The worker pricked another row of holes here and added another narrow braid of cloth stitch.
9. Space between Madonna's head and halo, filled with plaits.

Braids: Cloth Stitch
         Little Fishes
         Spot Spiders

Fillings: Plaited Bars
         Half Stitch

This piece of work shows how effective a small amount of decoration can be.

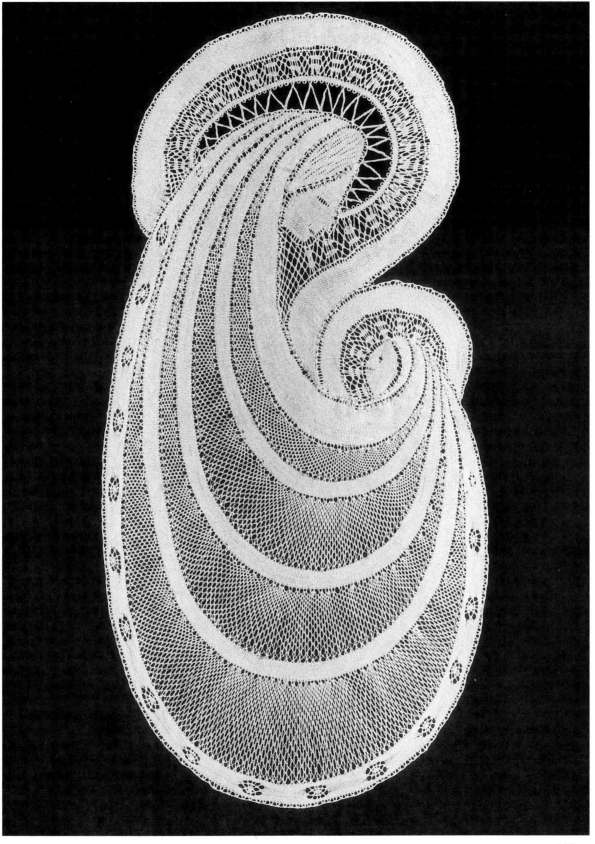

Sea Monster

An original design worked by Jane Read.
Thread: Copley Marshall No. 80

Start at the chin and work Cloth Divisions around
the outer edge of the mouth. Every pinhole on the
inside of the mouth needs to be worked as a blind
pin. Mittens in Half Stitch was used to decorate
the frilly parts of the monster and the beard. When
working the Figure-of-Eight on the tight curves it is
necessary to omit one repeat of part of the pattern
on the inner edge (ie the weavers were worked once
only through the trail).

   In the narrowest sections, the trail of the
Meander-in-Braid can be reduced to two pairs.

Braids: Cloth Divisions 3
         Mittens in Half Stitch
         Figure-of-Eight 3
         Meander-in-Braid 1

To provide for the greater variety of braids that
might be selected for this pattern, it is recommended that it be enlarged slightly.

See pricking, page 112

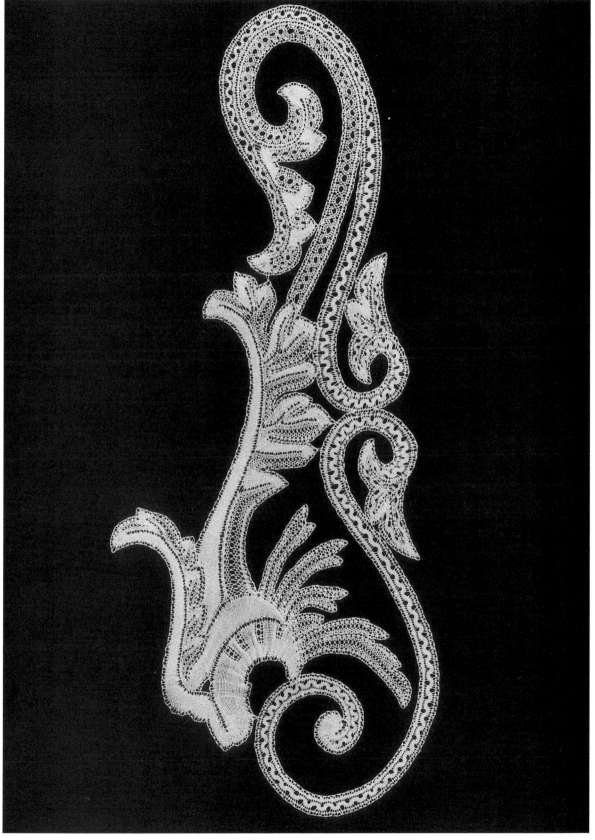

Sea Monster

Woman with Flower

Woman with Flower

An original design, based on a Chinese paper cut and worked by Lucy Kincaid.
Thread: Copley Marshall No. 80

ORDER OF WORKING

1. *Shawl:* Start at arm side with a false footing. Work towards waist. Lay the pairs to one side when the point is reached to be sewn in later.
2. *Hand and sleeve:* (holding flower) From finger tips to top of sleeve. Use a false footing extension at the wrist. (See page 18.) The sleeve and hand can be worked separately if preferred, in which case, work the sleeve first and then the hand.
3. Sew in the pairs laid aside from the shawl.
4. *Cummerbund:* Including the tiny piece tucked in under the hand.
5. *Lapels of gown:* From shoulder to waist.
6. *Hair:* (Both sections.) Work small wisp with ten stick. Ribbon put in with a two-pair filling (the crossing worked as a tally).
7. *Face and neck:* From forehead to base of neck. Twists to indicate chin.
8. *Extension of shawl:* (over arm with flower). From the bottom, upwards.
9. *Central panel of skirt:* From bottom to waist. Start with false footing. Use support pins.
10. *Back section of skirt:* From bottom upwards. Turn the pillow to get the correct angle of working.
11. *The underskirt:* Worked in half stitch.
12. *Last section of skirt.*
13. *Remainder of shawl:* From bottom upwards.
14. *Other hand and sleeve:* From finger tips to top of sleeve. Twists to indicate fingers. An extended false footing to get extra pairs for sleeve.
15. *The flower.*

Top sewings can be used to advantage in this piece.

Braids: Cloth Stitch
       Half Stitch
       Italian Fish
       Fish with Two Horizontals
       Ribbon

Filling: Two-pair crossing (with tallies)

Seaweed

An original design worked by Patricia Read.
Thread: Copley Marshall No. 80

The mat was designed for an experiment with larger holes, based on the method for Hole 1 but working the weavers into the hole several times. Not only does this enlarge the hole but it enables the sharp curves to be turned decoratively.

The braid is in five sections and these have been numbered in order of working. Begin the first braid where the holes are circled.

Braids: Mittens in Half Stitch
            Hole 1 (enlarged version)
            Zigzag Holes
            Meander-in-Braid 1

Fillings: Valenciennes
           Cobweb
           Half Stitch
           Cane Ground
           Valenciennes with picots. (For picots see page 59)
           Picot Bars

Note: The picot bars are a variation on those shown in Chapter Four. They were made with the weaver pair and the edge pair and were worked while the rest of the work *was in progress.*

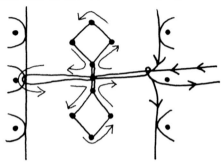

If it is decided to work picots in this way, the necessary pinholes must be pricked before work commences. Mark them on your pattern and prick at the same time as the rest of the pricking. This also applies to the extra picots on the edge of the piece. Instructions for working these will be found on page 60. For ordinary purl picots see page 147.

See pricking, page 118

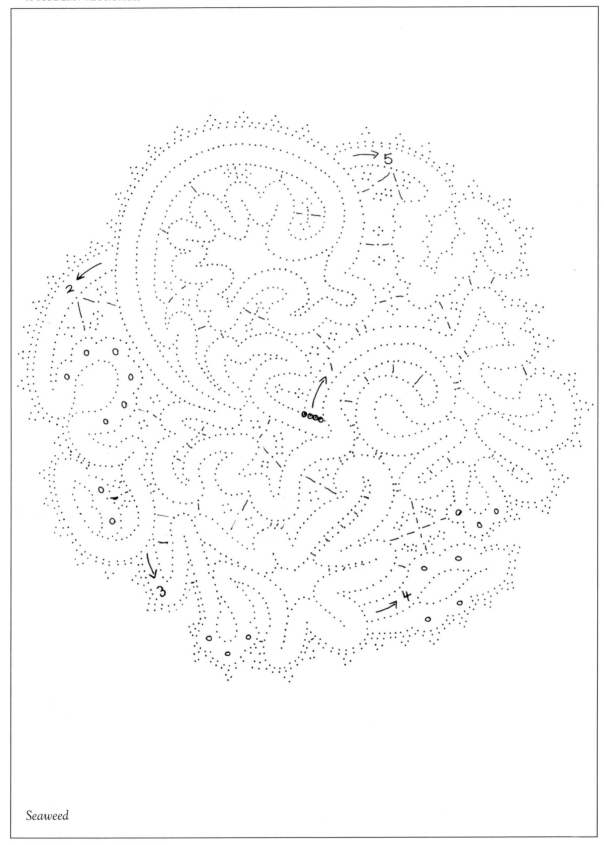

Seaweed

Cockatoo

Cockatoo

An original design worked by Hazel Goatham.
Thread: Brok No. 100

ORDER OF WORKING

1. *Eye.*
2. Outer eye ring.
3. Inner eye ring. (Filling)
4. *Top of head:* Worked as a continuous braid.
5. *Beak:* Upper, then lower.
6. Remainder of face (chin).
7. *Crest feathers:* From tips, towards head.
8. *Right wing:* Larger of the two wings.
9. *Right foot and leg.*
10. *Body:* From chin to tail.
11. *Left wing.*
12. *Left foot:* Part which is over branch.
13. *Branch:* All sections.
14. Finish feet.
15. *Tail:* From tips towards body. Largest feather first. Then the two on either side of it. The remainder, from the branch towards those already worked.

Braids: Half Stitch with twists and Cloth Stitch
  passives
  Cloth Stitch
  Cloth Stitch and twist variations
  Spot Spider
  Basketweave
  Horseshoes
  Some invented by the worker

Filling: Layered Gauze

Layered Gauze

No pins. Diagonal joins x t x. Horizontal pair twisted three times between joins, then one thread over and one thread under each join as it passes it. Horizontal pairs worked alternately to left and right.

Note: Either substitute braids from Chapter Three or do as this worker did, and experiment yourself.

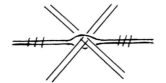

The Sisters

An original design worked by Hazel Goatham.
Thread: Brok No. 100

Prick in fillings before starting.

ORDER OF WORKING

SMALL GIRL FIRST
 1. *Headband.*
 2. *Hair:* All except braid on the right side of face. (Worker's left.)
 3. *Face:* From chin to hairline.
 4. *Bodice:* Fancy braids first.
 5. *Neck.*
 6. Rest of hair.
 7. *Left sleeve:* Outer braid first, then the inner one.
 8. *Left hand:* Twists for fingers.
 9. *Skirt:* Cloth stitch braids first, then the fancy panels. Outside edges worked in ten stick. Worked from the bottom, upwards.
10. *Pantaloons:* From the bottom towards the skirt.
11. *Feet:* From toe to heel.
12. *Socks.*

THE LARGER GIRL
 1. *Hair:* Top braid curling towards left.
 2. *Hair:* Braid falling behind shoulder on the right side. From parting until level with the eyes. Leave pairs to one side.
 3. *Face:* Chin to hair line.
 4. *Bodice:* Outer braids first, then the inner filling.
 5. *Neck.*
 6. Finish hair on both sides.
 7. *Skirt:* Ten stick outline. Basketweave braids first, then filling. (Note the angle at which this filling has been worked.)
 8. *Petticoat:* Worked with purl picots along edge.
 9. *Shoes:* From toe to heel.
10. *Stockings.*
11. *Sleeves:* Outer braid, then inner one.
12. *Hands:* From finger tips to wrists.

Braids: Meander-in-Braid
         Basketweave
         Figure-of-Eight 3
         Cloth Divisions
         Cloth Stitch with twists

Fillings: Half Stitch
          Pinwheel
          Spider with Torchon Ground (skirt)

Spider with Torchon Ground

This is worked with pinholes at centre of Spiders. All joins x t x. Twists as indicated on diagram.

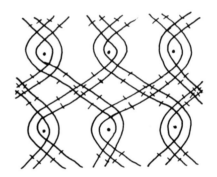

The Sisters

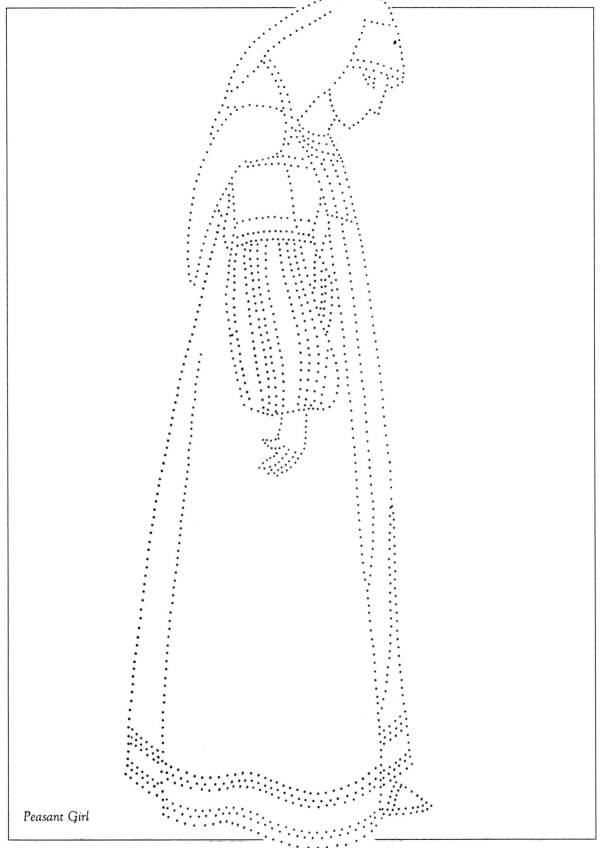

Peasant Girl

Peasant Girl

A design, based on a drawing by Ivan Bilibin (1876–1942), a Russian illustrator of international fame. It was worked by Lucy Kincaid, and shows how braid can be combined with other techniques.

Prick in the fillings of your choice before starting work (use a fine pricker).

ORDER OF WORKING
1. *Headscarf:* a) Back worked in half stitch. b) Front. Narrow cloth stitch braid first, then filling.
2. *Necklace:* From front to back.
3. *Sleeve:* a) Folds in ten stick. b) Lower half worked from wrist to elbow, made up of a number of narrow braids worked without an outside edge pair, and joined with edge sewings. c) Upper half worked *across* the sleeve using braids and a filling. (Work over the top of the ten stick fold across middle of section.)
4. *Hand:* From finger tips to wrist. Each finger a separate braid. Use top sewings where fingers overlap.
5. *Head:* From forehead to base of neck.
6. *Bodice:* Narrow cloth stitch braids, worked without outside edge pairs.
7. *Skirt:* a) inside fold line at back of skirt. Tenstick for this fold line turning it into a narrow cloth stitch braid along bottom of skirt then turning it back to tenstick for front fold and carrying it straight into inner decorated braid. b) Outer front in decorated braid. c) Remaining outside edges in tenstick, turning into narrow braid and sewn off into middle section of skirt. d) Put in a narrow cloth stitch braid across bottom of skirt to match the lower one. Put in the decorated braid. e) Put the filling in the main part of the skirt using top sewings round sleeve and hand. Note how the tenstick can be sewn into on both sides, thus giving a raised edge on one side, and a flat edge on the other.
8. *Shoe:* From toe to heel.

Braids: Ovals
          Cloth Stitch (without an edge pair)
          Cross-over 2

Fillings: Two pair filling
          Twisted Half Stitch ground (Skirt)
          Fishes variation (Sleeve)
          Fishes variation (Headscarf)

Twisted Half Stitch ground

All joins x t t pin x t.

 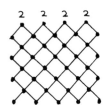

Fishes variation (Sleeve)

At pins, x t x pin x t x. All other joins x t x. Twists as indicated on diagram.

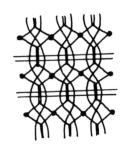 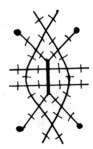

Fishes variation (Headscarf)

All joins x t x. Twists as indicated on diagram.

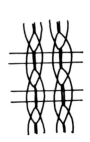 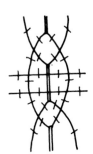

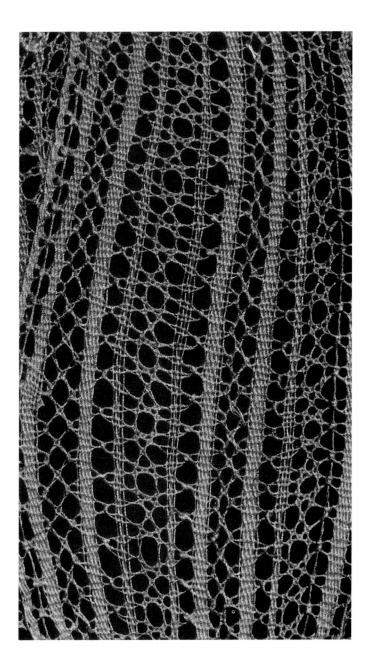

Using different braids to create an over-all fabric

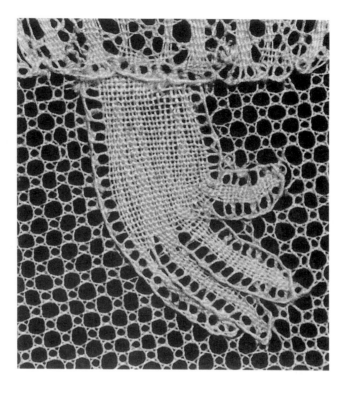

Start at the finger tips

Owl

Owl

An original design worked by Hazel Goatham.
Thread: Brok No. 100

Join the two sections of the pricking.

ORDER OF WORKING

1. *Face mask:* (moustache and eyebrows.)
2. *Eye patches:* Eyes left as spaces. Pupils worked with tallies.
3. *Beak area:* A triangular raised tally for the beak, with braid worked over the top.
4. *The remainder of the face.* (The four braids which form the cheeks.)
5. *Ruff:* (The braid which starts under the 'chin' and goes round over the top of the head). Fill in tiny spaces at top of head.
6. *Right wing:* (Worker's left) The three long feathers at the top, starting with the upper one. Worked from tips, towards head. (Use top sewings.)
7. *Small feathers of right wing:* Worked from tips towards long feathers. Narrow braids first. Order of working from feather 'a' towards the wing tip. Then from feather 'b' towards the body.
8. *Body:* From ruff to bottom of right leg.
9. *Left leg:* From top downwards.
10. *Feet:* From claws towards body.
11. *Tail:* From tips towards body.
12. *Left wing:* The three top feathers. Start with the upper feather and work from tips towards body. Work the smaller feathers from body towards wing tip.

Braids: Fishes
Meander-in-Braid 1
Basketweave
Archway
Half Stitch
Buds – 4-pin
Hole 1
Cloth Divisions 2
Cloth Stitch with twists
Other variations arrived at as work was in progress.

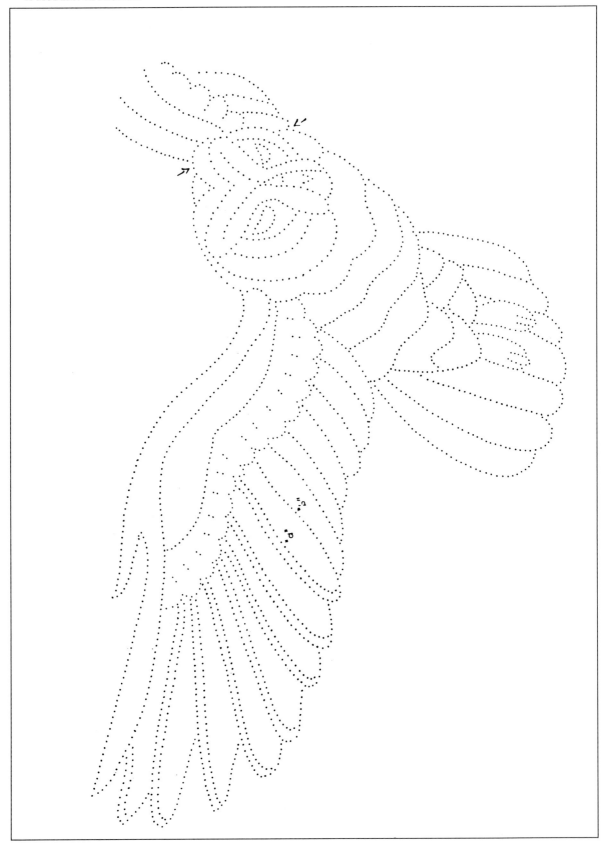

Owl

The Mermaid

An original design worked by Lucy Kincaid.
Thread: Retors d'Alsace No. 40

Before starting work prick in the filling for the sea and the sky. Use a finer pricker for this to avoid confusion with the braid holes.

ORDER OF WORKING

1. *Frame:* Mark on the pattern where divisions are to come.
2. *The two sets of double waves:* The bottom one of each pair first. Use top sewings.
3. *Both fish:* Top tail fin, round body, finish at bottom tail fin.
4. *Mermaid's hair:* Start at top, finish at points. Use edge sewings.
5. *Face:* Tie the leader at nose tip. (See note on working eye at foot of page.)
6. *Hand and arm:* Start with hand, sew arm off into hair. Use a single pair to bridge gap between arm and hair afterwards, as explained in Chapter Four.
7. *Mermaid's tail:* Start at tip of tail fins, then combine braids to make tail. Combine tail braids to work body. Alternatively, work the fins, tail and body in one piece. If working separately lay each set of bobbins to one side until needed.
8. *Rock:* Tenstick outline with basketweave filling. Use support pins. Take or add pairs two at a time. This would work just as well using fewer pairs.
9. *Small waves.*
10. *Horizon line:* Tenstick, with pinholes on the sea side.
11. *Bird:* a) Body. Start at tail, finish at beak. b) Wings. Start by sewing into body. Finish at tips. Weaver tied at wing peaks.
12. *Sea:* Worked in Tulle du Puy. The pillow was turned so that the picture was on its side when this was worked. Use a mixture of top and edge sewings. (See photograph.)
13. *Sky:* Trolley net. Pillow turned so that the picture was upside down. Where convenient, pairs were carried across the back of the hair and the bird.

Braids: Meander-in-Braid 2
Ribbon
Cloth Divisions
Archway
Cloth Stitch

Fillings: Tulle du Puy
Trolley Net
Basketweave (with tenstick outline)

The worker experimented with braids in this piece of work.

Meander-in-Braid: Worked with one straight passive. The weaver taken across to the opposite side on every other row. A turning stitch worked on alternate rows.

Ribbon: In the original all sets of two pairs cross on the same row. In this variation they cross alternately, on alternate rows. Also areas of cloth stitch were introduced while work was in progress.

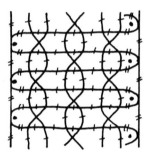

Archway: Worked with fewer pairs, giving four legs only.

Mermaid's Eye: Working away from the hair edge, twist the weavers twice over the selected spot (a pinhole in the pattern) and continue to the profile edge.

On the left take the weaver back to the place where it was twisted on the previous row. Work a turning stitch with the last passive pair before the twists, work back to the left edge. Leave weavers at pin.

On the right sew a new pair into the next pinhole to be worked. Take it as the weaver and work towards the centre. Make a turning stitch with the last passive pair before the twists. Work back to the right edge, sew into the same hole and leave as a passive. Work a reverse half stitch with the two pairs either side of the centre gap. Find the weavers and continue, taking care to pull the passives into place carefully.

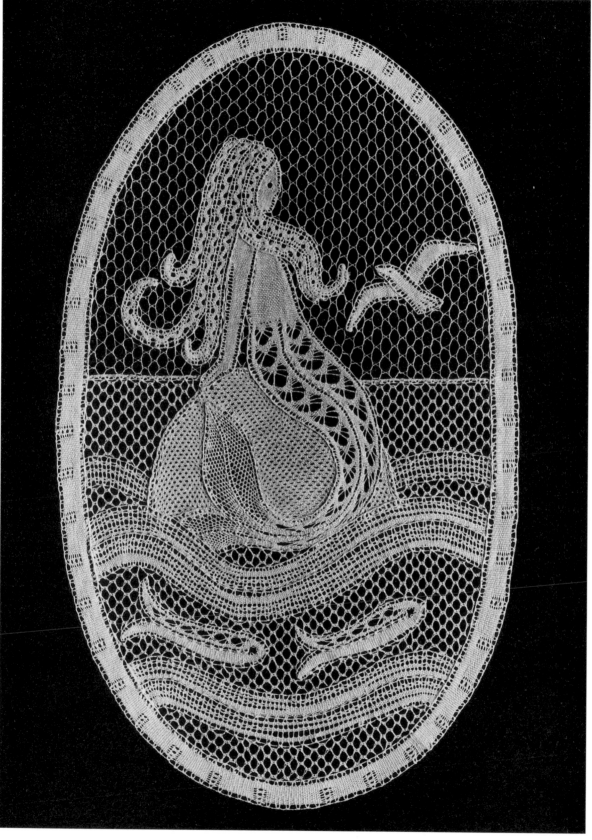

Tulle du Puy

Pairs sewn in, in sets of two. Twist each pair once.
Join the pairs at each crossing with x t x pin x t x t.

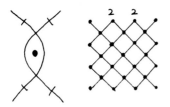

The Mermaid

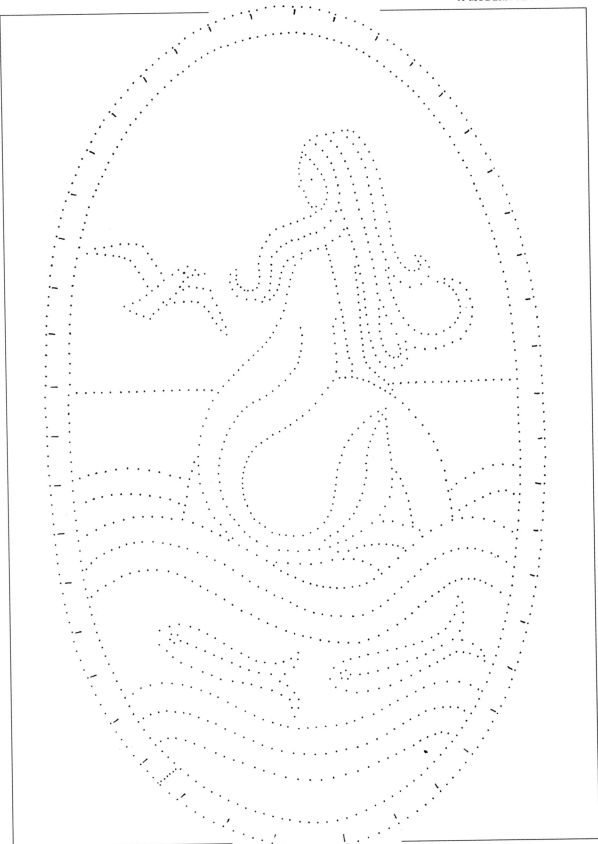

CHAPTER 7

Making a Pattern

Having found a picture or a design which you want to turn into a pattern, how do you go about it? Whether the picture or design is large or small, complicated or simple, the procedure is the same.

Preparation

You will need:

a) the original picture. If you can draw it so much the better, but a picture from any source, even a newspaper, can be used. It is far easier to judge the width of your braid if the picture is the size you intend the finished lace to be. Enlarge or reduce it by the photocopying method, *after* the first tracing has been made.

b) a tracing pad. Be prepared to use this freely. Do not detach the top sheet. Slip the picture you are tracing under it. This will hold it firmly in position.

c) a pencil which will rub out easily, but keep its point reasonably well.

d) a soft rubber.

e) a coloured pen (extra fine tip).

f) time and patience.

g) the intention to enjoy what you are doing.

Method

Stage 1

Begin by making a tracing of your original picture.

Do not think about braids at all at this point, though if your design naturally falls into braids, so much the better. Concentrate instead on the main lines of the design. Imagine you are tracing it to make a picture for a small child to colour in. Enlarge or reduce at this stage if necessary.

Put aside your original picture and turn to your tracing. *Turn it over so that the pencil line is on the*

underside. This is important. As you work you will want to rub out. With the main pencil lines on the underneath side of the tracing you can revise your work without losing your original lines. Do this at each stage of the tracing process.

Stage 2

Some of the lines you have traced will end in mid-air. Extend these lines to meet up with other lines. Smooth out saw-edged lines. Make sure each shape within the design has an outline around it. You will then have a drawing composed of shapes which fit together like a jigsaw.

Stage 3

Keep re-tracing your picture, making it simpler each time, using a fresh sheet of tracing paper when it becomes necessary. The aim is to eliminate as many of the smaller pieces as possible and to incorporate them into the larger shapes. When you are satisfied that the picture is as simple as you can make it, you are ready to think of the *braid*.

Stage 4

Braids can be all shapes and sizes as long as they each have a beginning, middle and end, and can, as a general rule, be worked with approximately 16 pairs, or less. Wider braids, in which more pairs are used, are sometimes an important element in a design. (See illustration on page 114.) These should however be kept to a minimum as they are more difficult to work and the use of support pins becomes essential.

Some of the shapes in your design will be braid shape already, some will divide into braids easily and some will require more thought. You can now understand the point of working to the size one wants the finished lace to be. Use your imagination and do not always decide on the obvious, but look at what has been done elsewhere.

Make proper use of the various ways of filling in the spaces within a design (see Chapter Four) and consider the occasional use of tenstick outlines which can be 'filled in' later.

If there is an essential feature, for example an eye, make sure it is in a position where it can be worked. The bird's eye was placed in the middle of a braid so that it could be worked as a hole. The fish eye was made by leaving a space where the braid loops back on itself.

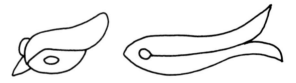

Do not leave this kind of decision until work is in progress. You may find you have given yourself a problem which is difficult to resolve.

When you have worked out all the braid shapes take a final, clean tracing. Check that every braid in the jigsaw has a place to start and a place to finish. Consider *how* and *where* it will start and finish. Make sure that every space within your design is accounted for. Do not leave *any* awkward decisions until work is in progress. Work out how you will tackle tricky places at *this* stage. Now is the time to alter your pattern if you cannot see a way out of a problem. Far better to tackle a problem at this stage and proceed with confidence, than to abandon the work later on.

You should now have a tracing on which you know what every line and space means. Put this tracing under the top sheet of your pad. Fasten it securely. Double-sided photomounts are very good. You are now ready to prepare your pricking.

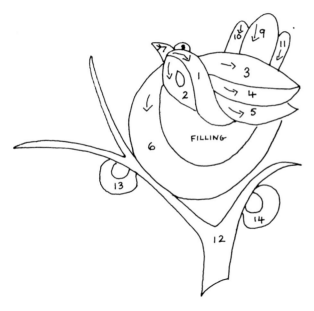

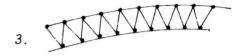

3.

3. Put in the second line of dots.

Where two braids touch and have a line of holes in common, dot the centre line first.

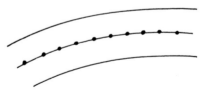

Where two braids touch for a short distance, mark in one of the braids as normal. On the second braid work backwards, and then forwards, from the point where they touch.

Stage 5

PREPARING A PRICKING

In deciding how far apart you should put the dots look at the prickings in Chapter Six and you will see that it is largely a matter of personal choice. Generally speaking, the finer the thread the closer together the holes should be. Practise by dotting on a piece of graph paper. This helps to build up a dotting rhythm, which in turn helps to regulate the spacing between dots.

When working braid, especially one with curves, it is inevitable that on occasions a back-stitch (or 'blind' pin) will be necessary. Decorated braid must breathe and the pattern must be seen clearly. Back-stitches tend to crowd a pattern so the fewer there are the better it will be. They can be kept to a minimum by careful plotting of the weavers. Dot one complete braid at a time.

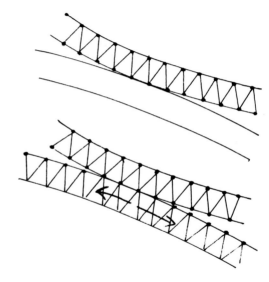

Where the short end of one braid joins the broadside of another, make sure the holes of the one braid meet with the holes of the other. Where there is a series of curving braids placed side by side (as in a skirt), work from the centre outwards or the holes will be too close together on one side, and too far apart on the other.

1.

1. Mark the dots, in pencil, along one side of the braid.

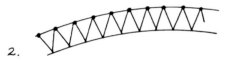

2.

2. Draw in the path of the weavers, turning the tracing pad towards yourself all the time as though you are actually working the lace.

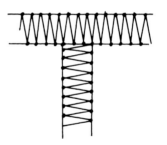

When all the weaver lines are drawn and all the
dots are in position, go over the dots with a
coloured pen. This distinguishes them from stray
pencil marks. Rub out all the pencil marks, and if
necessary make a clean tracing. At this stage make
a copy of your pattern by the photocopying
method. If you have a disaster while pricking you
will not have to begin all over again.

Faces need special care: Make two parallel lines
across the face, one through the eyes, one through
the mouth. Turn the face so that these two lines
become the path of the weavers. Draw the weavers
in, in both directions. Put in the dots, making sure
that where the face braid meets another braid they
match exactly. Back-stitches distort a face. Mark
the position of the eyes and mouth on the pattern
and put an arrow to remind yourself of the angle of
working.

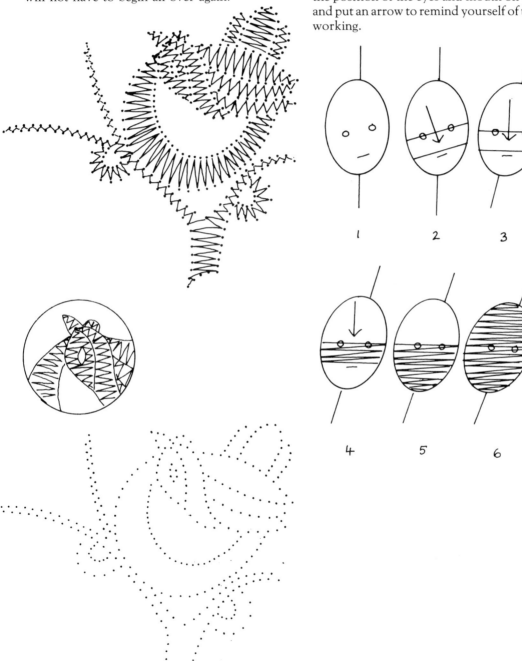

Stage 6

MAKING THE PRICKING

Put a clean piece of tracing paper over the dotted pattern and prick through this. This might seem a waste of tracing paper, but in fact, it makes pricking easier, because it shows very clearly where you have already pricked. Once you have tried it you will never prick any other way. When pricking try not to stop in the middle of a line of dots. When the hand has been taken off, say to wax, restart by going into the last couple of holes pricked to get back to the continuity of line. This helps avoid that 'juddering' effect which is, alas, so easy to achieve.

When pricking areas of ground or filling, no matter how small, work them out on graph paper first. When the main part of the pricking is finished, slide the graph paper between the pricking and the tracing. Manoeuvre it into position, bearing in mind the direction in which it is to be worked. *Re-pin it using the same holes.* This is important as the holes on the tracing and the holes on the pricking card underneath *must* match if the filling is to be put in accurately. For smaller areas, cut the graph paper to a convenient size and slide it into position without moving the pins at all. Use a finer pricker for the filling so that there is a difference between the filling and the braids. This avoids confusion when working. Go over the filling holes with a larger pricker when you are ready to work them.

When your pricking is finished you may be dissatisfied with it because
a) some of the holes are out of alignment;
b) you have pricked a section badly;
c) you have had a change of mind about part of the design.
Do not abandon the pricking.

REVISING A PRICKING

Take a piece of sticky, brown paper parcel tape and stick it over the offending area. It is possible to cut a piece small enough to cover *one* incorrect pinhole (manoeuvre it into position with a pin after you have moistened it). It is worth taking the trouble to do this. To reprick without using brown paper results in a 'mess' of pinholes in which it is impossible to tell which is the correct one. Mark in the revised pinholes with a pencil, then prick them. Small revisions can be done with the eye. Larger revisions need more care.

Retrace the section to be revised, from the original tracing, making the tracing a little larger than the brown paper patch. Put in the revised dots. Because the new tracing is larger than the

brown patch it can be matched accurately with the pricking underneath. Make sure it is in the right position, pin it down and re-prick. If patching in the middle of a design, pin the patch down through the pricked pinholes at the edges of the patch, *using lace pins.*

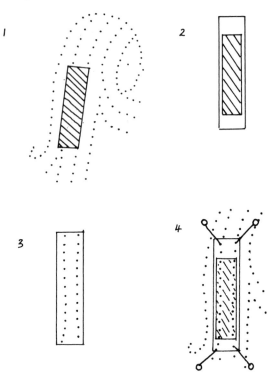

Patching
1. *Stick brown paper patch over incorrect pinholes.*
2. *Cut a piece of tracing paper slightly larger than patch.*
3. *Retrace dots from original pattern or redraw them.*
4. *Match tracing with pricking at edges of patch. Pin, using lace pins, through tracing and into pricked holes underneath.*
    Prick holes into patch.   Remove tracing.

Use the brown paper method when putting in an extra pinhole, ie when three pinholes are needed in a space now taken by two. Cover the two pinholes with a strip of brown paper, and re-space the holes evenly. Keep a small roll of brown paper in your work-tin at all times.

Small revisions can be made on the pillow while work is in progress. Do not attempt a large scale revision whilst work is in progress unless you are very confident, and only then if it is absolutely essential. Finally, mark in weaver lines where they will assist with the working.

The balance of plain and decorated braid

This is an important factor in a design, particularly in the more traditional patterns where plain braid can enhance the appearance of a decorated one. Plan where the areas of plain and decorated braid are to be before you begin work and mark them on your pattern and your pricking.

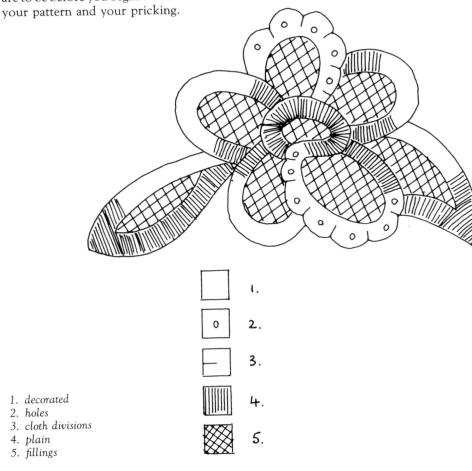

1. decorated
2. holes
3. cloth divisions
4. plain
5. fillings

You have spent a lot of time working on your design and pricking and are now ready to work the lace. If you are tempted to change your pattern whilst work is in progress, remember how much thought you have already given it, and have confidence in the decisions you have already made.

CHAPTER 8

Further Notes on Technique

Adding pairs

Adding one pair

Work to the pin, twist the weaver twice. When the pin is in, but before the edge stitch is worked, pick up the new pair with one bobbin in each hand. Slide the thread up, under, the weaver pair and lay the bobbins back over the pillow. Complete the edge stitch. Bring the new pair down into the work and lay it beside the first passive pair. The new pair is now the second passive pair. Putting it in this position ensures that the outside passive remains continuous.

Adding two pairs at one pinhole

Add the first pair as described above. When the edge stitch has been worked but the pin is still unclosed, take a second pair up and under the weaver and lay it back over the pillow. Leave it. Take the weaver through the braid to the opposite side and work the edge stitch. Before the weaver is returned bring the second new pair down into the work, again laying it beside the first passive pair. The second new pair is now lying between the first passive pair and the first new pair. Return to the weaver and continue.

Adding pairs in half stitch

This is done in the same way, except that the new pair is laid between the two threads of the first passive pair. Make sure the threads are crossed in readiness for the half stitch before work is continued.

Adding pairs in the centre of a braid

Just occasionally it is necessary to thicken a braid. For example, when an open braid changes into a denser one. Extra pairs can be laid round pins in the centre of the braid, thus:

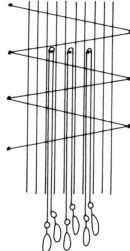

Do not remove the pins until absolutely necessary. If these pairs are pulled too tightly a hole will appear. Use this method sparingly.

Taking pairs out

Taking pairs out in cloth stitch

Simply lay the pairs back and cut them off later. Always take pairs out on the inside of a curve. *Never* take the first passive pair as this is the pair which gives the edge of the braid its continuous line. If a number of pairs are to be taken out over a short distance, 'stagger' them across the entire width of the braid.

Taking pairs out in half stitch

Work to within two pairs of the edge pair. Take the weavers through these two pairs in cloth stitch, and then work the edge stitch. Before returning, take the two centre threads of the two pairs worked in cloth stitch. Tie them together, taking care not to pull too tightly, and lay them back over the pillow. They can be cut off later. Cross the two remaining threads and continue.

Taking pairs out in decorated braid

If the pairs to be taken out are straight passives they can be laid back. If they are part of the decoration they are best taken out at the pin. Sometimes these pairs can be laid back, at other times they must be sewn into the pinhole and tied. This is done at the worker's discretion. It sometimes helps in the continuity of the decoration to take out two pairs at a time. That is, two pairs in one place, rather than one pair in two different places. Before any pairs are taken out of decorated braid, be sure they have worked their full quota of the decoration.

Backstitch or 'blind' pin

Sometimes there are more pinholes on one side of a braid than on the other. This means that some pinholes must be worked twice. To do this, take the weaver to the hole where the backstitch is to be made. Twist the weaver twice, but do not work the edge stitch. Leave the edge pair to one side. Put the pin under the weaver, and return the weaver to the opposite side, where the usual edge stitch is worked. Take the weaver back to the backstitch side. At the pinhole twist the weaver and work the usual edge stitch with the edge pair. Take the pin from the hole worked on the previous row. Replace the pin in the same hole, at the same time gently pushing the loop made on the previous row to one side. Close the pin and continue, remembering to pull the passives well into the pin for several more rows.

When to make a backstitch/'blind' pin

Always work with the braid coming towards yourself. Whenever the weavers start to go uphill, make a backstitch to bring it back to the right path. See the diagram. One of the few exceptions to this rule occurs in Meander-in-Braid.

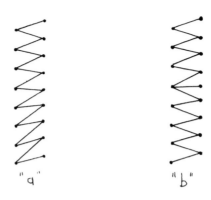

Broken threads

What to do when a thread breaks and leaves a short end

If this happens in cloth stitch (this includes any small area) another thread is laid in. Take *one* wound bobbin, make a loop in the end of the thread and either pin it to the pillow, or loop it round a pin already in the work. Lay the thread where the broken thread would have fallen and continue as usual. The ends can be cut off later.

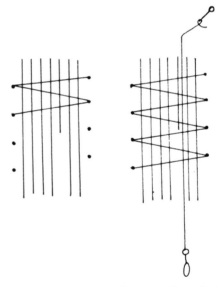

When this happens elsewhere it is best dealt with by joining the broken thread with a weavers' knot (see note further on) and then undoing enough of the work to double the broken thread with a new thread. To do this the new thread is laid in as above. Then the thread with the knot and the new thread are worked together for a short while. This can be done either by fixing the two bobbins together with an elastic band or one of the tags used to close plastic bags, or by cutting the knotted thread of sufficient length to wind round the bobbin with the new thread for a short distance. It helps to twist these two threads together. When enough work has been done to hold the thread securely (about 1–2cm) the knotted thread can be unwound and laid back across the pillow. It can be cut off later.

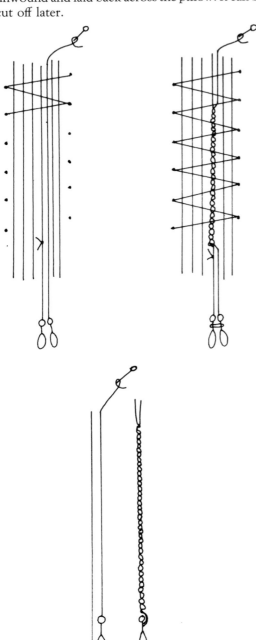

passive (see note further on). The passive can then be doubled up with a new thread and renewed. If a thread breaks when tying off after sewing, tie the remaining thread of the pair to the thread lying next to it.

Hanging pairs on/open

This is sometimes described as hanging round a pin, and is the term used when pairs are hung inside one another as in diagram 'a'.

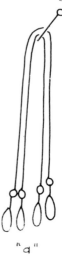

"a"

Hanging pairs side by side

Sometimes pairs which are hung round a pin at the beginning of the work have pairs sewn into them at the end of the work. In order to keep the loops separate, the pairs are hung side by side, as in diagram 'b'.

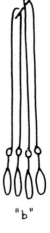

"b"

If a weaver breaks the work must be undone far enough for the weaver to be exchanged with a

Changing a weaver thread

Sometimes one of the weaver threads starts to run out when there is only a small amount of work still to be done, or it becomes worn and is in danger of breaking. At an inconspicuous place (usually just before working the pin) work the first half of the stitch as usual. Make an extra twist so that the short/worn thread is exchanged with a passive thread. It takes a little practice to exchange the correct one at first. Close the pin and proceed as usual. Until the old weaver thread has settled into its new position take extra care when pulling up the passives. Any worn or short thread can be exchanged in this way. It can then be moved to a position where it is less vulnerable, where it can be laid back, or where it can be renewed less noticeably.

Tying the weaver

Passives are liable to pull away from any peak that occurs along the edge of a braid, thus causing an unsightly gap. They can be kept under control by tying the weaver pair. This is done *after* the pinhole at the point of the peak has been worked. Tie the weaver pair once, after it has passed through the first passive pair on the return journey.

Purl picots

Picots give a decorative edge and are an optional extra. Unless used for special effect in modern style work, they should only be made on the outer edge of the work. If picots are required, a second row of holes should be pricked on the outside and very close (about 2mm) to the existing row of holes of the design. These new holes have the effect of widening the braid slightly and the original row of holes is not used. It will be noticed that the making of the purl picot takes up this extra width, enabling the line of the braid to remain smooth and not to become indented where the picots start and finish. Seeing the double row of holes also serves as a reminder that picots should be made. It is wise, therefore, to prick all the picot holes before work commences. If it should happen on completion of a piece of work that some picots have been missed, it is possible to add them before the lace is removed from the pillow. To do this, sew in one pair of bobbins to the pinhole alongside the first purl picot to be worked. Twist and make the picot in the usual way, sew the pair back into the same hole and tie once. Sew the same pair into the next hole and work the next picot. Again sew into the same hole. Continue as necessary, finally tying off three times.

To make a purl picot

Work the weavers through the edge pair, twist the edge pair once and leave. Twist the weavers five times (eight times if the thread is very fine, say, 140 or 180). Catch up the outside thread with a pin, (this is explained on page 59 if you are unfamiliar with picots) and pass the second bobbin round the pin in a clockwise direction if the picot is made on the left (anti-clockwise if made on the right), and watch the twists spin round the pin as the threads are drawn up together against the pin. Work cloth stitch and twist with the edge pair.

To make a false picot

Hang two pairs open round a pin. Twist them five times, then work them together with cloth stitch. These pairs can now be carried into the work.

Support pins

When working a wide braid the weaver will sometimes sag. This puts a strain on it. If pulled too tightly there is a risk it will snap. To counterbalance this, the use of support pins is advised. Holes for these are pricked as they are needed. As the weaver is taken across the work, put a pin *underneath* it, in line with the pin just worked at the edge of the braid. This will take the weight off the weaver and make it easier (and safer) to pull it up. If the braid is very wide put in more than one support pin. Remove them from the work as soon as possible. Just occasionally a weaver will ride up, in which case place a support pin *above* it, to hold it down.

Tallies and leaves

These are used only occasionally in this kind of lace. Follow the diagrams. All are worked with two pairs. Do not let any weight fall on the weaver thread while work is in progress as this will pull the tally or leaf out of shape.

To make a square tally

Begin by twisting both pairs. Take the *second thread* from the left, and using this as the weaver work it over and under towards the right. Then continue,

still using the same weaver
* over, under, over to the left
under, over, under to the right *.
Repeat from * to * for the required length. Twist the pairs to finish. The threads at the side of the tally govern its shape, therefore, keep these 'open' to the required width.

To make a leaf

A leaf is worked in the same way as a tally except it is begun and finished with a cloth stitch. This pulls the pairs together and gives the typical leaf shape. Use the threads at the sides to control the shape of the leaf. Do not start tapering off until the leaf is three quarters complete.

To make a triangular tally

Start as for a leaf, and finish as for a square tally. (Or in reverse order.)

Basic spider

A spider in braid is worked in the same way as any other spider, except that instead of a pin being placed at the centre of it, a turning stitch is made with the last two pairs of the first half.

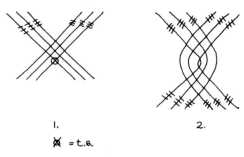

1.

2.

$\boldsymbol{\bowtie}$ = t.s.

To work the first half of a spider each pair is twisted (usually three times). All the pairs on the left pass through all the pairs on the right in cloth stitch. Make a turning stitch with the last two pairs to be worked. The first half is now complete.

To work the second half of the spider again pass all the pairs on the left through all the pairs on the right in cloth stitch. Twist all pairs (usually three times). The spider is now complete.

Basic fish

There are numerous variations on the arrangement of the fish themselves, and the pairs linking them together. It is a fruitful area for experimentation. There are two interesting examples in the illustration on page 127. Each fish is composed of two pairs joined at the top with a cloth stitch. The horizontal pairs (which are worked from side to side of the braid or filling) pass through each fish in cloth stitch, with twists made before and after the fish. The fish is finished by working the two pairs together in cloth stitch. Experiment.

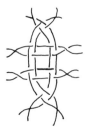

Tenstick

Though not strictly a braid, this can be used as one, especially for small detail. It can also be used to outline a shape which is later filled in with another stitch. It is usually worked with five pairs (thus the name tenstick) but it can be worked with anything from four to eight pairs. It is worked with holes on one side only, and is pricked as a single line of holes.

Starting tenstick at a free end

Hang five pairs round a pin. x t x t t the two pairs on the pinhole side. Take the inside pair as the weavers. Work it through the next two pairs in cloth stitch, then through the third pair with a turning stitch. Take the second pair from the edge as the new weaver and return to the pinhole side (pinning under two pairs). Continue in this way, taking care to pull up properly after each row is worked.

Starting tenstick where it is joined to another part of the work

Sew five pairs into the appropriate holes. Do not twist them. x t x t t the two pairs on the pinhole side, and proceed as before.

Weavers' knot

This is used to join two threads when one of them is very short. With skill even an end a centimetre long can be caught and tied. Sometimes it helps to moisten this short end. Take the new thread and

make an ordinary Granny loop with it. (See the diagram.) Put this loop over the short thread. Pull the two ends coming from the loop at the same time, one towards the left, one towards the right, and give them a sharp jerk so that the loop is pulled tightly round the short thread. It can take two or three attempts to get it to catch. Trim the ends.

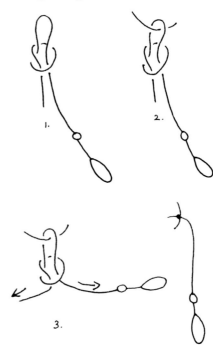

Bibliography

Cook, B. and Stott, G., *The Book of Bobbin Lace Stitches*, Batsford, 1980

Holéczyová, E., *Dentelles de notre temps*, Dessain et Tolra, 1978

Simeon, M., *The History of Lace*, Stainer & Bell, 1979, Dover Publications (Pictorial Archive Series)

Suppliers

United Kingdom

Alby Lace Museum
Cromer Road
Alby
Norfolk
NR11 7QE

Bedford Lace
4 Newnham Street
Bedford

Ann Brock
1 Ingham Close
Blake Hall Road
Mirfield
Yorkshire

Campden Needlecraft Centre
High Street
Chipping Campden
Gloucestershire

Chosen Crafts Centre
46 Winchcombe Street
Cheltenham
Gloucestershire
GL52 2ND

Margaret Clark
Mount Vernon
Lyme Road
Higher Poynton
Stockport
Cheshire
SK12 1TH

Leonie Cox
The Old School
Childswickham
Near Broadway
Worcs
WR12 7HD

J. and J. Ford
October Hill
Upper Way
Upper Longdon
Rugeley
Staffordshire
WS15 1QB

Framecraft
83 Hampstead Road
Handsworth Wood
Birmingham
B2L 1JA

Mr R. Gravestock
Highwood
Crews Hill
Alfrick
Worcestershire
WR6 5HF

Hepatica
82a Water Lane
Wilmslow
Cheshire

Frank Herring & Sons
27 High West Street
Dorchester
Dorset
DT1 1UP

Honiton Lace Shop
44 High Street
Honiton
Devon

D.J. Hornsby
149 High Street
Burton Latimer
Kettering
Northants
NN15 5RL

and

25 Manwood Avenue
Canterbury
Kent
CT2 7AH

Pastimes
24–6 West Street
Alresford
Hampshire

Jane's Pincushion
Wroxham Barns
Tunstead Road
Hoveton
Norwich
NR12 2QU

All branches of John Lewis

Lambourn Valley Cottage
   Industries
11 Oxford Street
Lambourn
Berks
RG16 7XS

Mace and Nairn
89 Crane Street
Salisbury
Wiltshire
SP1 2PY

Iris Martin
Farthing Cottage
Clickers Yard
Yardley Road
Olney
Bucks

Needle Work
Ann Bartlet
Bucklers Farm
Coggeshall
Essex CO6 1SB

The Needlewoman
21 Needless Abbey
off New Street
Birmingham
B2 5AE

T. Parker
124 Corhampton Road
Boscombe East
Bournemouth
BH6 5NZ

Dorothy Pearce
5 Fulshaw Avenue
Wilmslow
Cheshire
SK9 51A

Jane Playford
North Lodge
Church Close
West Runton
Norfolk
NR27 9QY

Christine Riley
53 Barclay Street
Stonehaven
Kincardineshire
Scotland

Pat Savory
Tanglewood
4 Sanden Close
Hungerford
Berks
RG17 0LB

Peter and Beverley Scarlett
Strupak
Hill Head
Coldwells
Ellon, Grampian

Ken and Pat Schultz
134 Wisbech Road
Thornley
Peterborough

J.S. Sear
Lacecraft Supplies
8 Hill View
Sherrington
Buckinghamshire

Sebalace
Waterloo Mills
Howden Road
Silsden
W. Yorks
BD2 0HA

A. Sells
49 Pedley Lane
Clifton
Shefford
Bedfordshire

Shireburn Lace
Finkle Court
Finkle Hill
Sherburn in Elmet
N. Yorks
LS25 6EB

Stephen Simpson
Avenham Road Works
Preston
Lancs

Stitches
Dovehouse Shopping Parade
Warwick Road
Olton
Solihull
West Midlands

S.M.P.
4 Garners Close
Chalfont St Peter
Bucks
SL9 0HB

Teazle Embroideries
35 Boothferry Road
Hull
North Humberside

Valley House Crafts Studios
Ruston
Scarborough
N. Yorks

George Walker
The Corner Shop
Rickinghall
Diss
Norfolk

George White
Delaheys Cottage
Thistle Hill
Knaresborough
N. Yorks
HG5 8LS

Bobbins

A.R. Archer
The Poplars
Shelland
Near Stowmarket
Suffolk
IP14 3DE

T. Brown
Temple Lane Cottage
Littledean
Cinderford
Gloucestershire

Bridge Bookshop
7 Bridge Street
Bath
Avon
B82 4AS

Stephen Cook
'Cottage Crafts'
6 Woodland Close
Flackwell Heath
Buckinghamshire
HP10 9EP

Chrisken Bobbins
26 Cedar Drive
Kingsclere
Newbury
Bucks
RG15 8TD

Malcolm J. Fielding
2 Northern Terrace
Moss Lane
Silverdale
Lancs
LA5 0ST

Richard Gravestock
Highwood
Crews Hill
Alfrick
Worcestershire
WR6 5HF

Larkfield Crafts
Hilary Rickitts
4 Island Cottages
Mapledurwell
Basingstoke
Hants
RG25 2LU

Lambourn Valley Cottage
  Industries
11 Oxford Street
Lambourn
Berks
RG16 7XS

T. Parker
124 Corhampton Road
Boscombe East
Bournemouth
BH6 5NZ

Bryn Phillips
'Pantglas'
Cellan
Dyfed
Lampeter
SA48 8JD

D.H. Shaw
47 Zamor Crescent
Thruscroft
Rotherham
S. Yorks
S66 9QD

Sizelands
1 Highfield Road
Winslow
Bucks
MK10 3QU

Christine and David Springett
21 Hillmorton Road
Rugby
Warwickshire
CV22 5DF

Richard Viney
Unit 7
Port Royal Street
Southsea
Hants
PO5 4NP

George White
Delaheys Cottage
Thistle Hill
Knaresborough
N. Yorks

Lace pillows

Newnham Lace Equipment
15 Marlowe Close
Basingstoke
Hants
RG 24 9DD

Books

Bridge Bookshop
7 Bridge Street
Bath
Avon
B82 4AS

Craft Bookcase
29 London Road
Sawbridgeworth
Herts
CM21 9EH

Christopher Williams
19 Morrison Avenue
Parkstone
Poole
Dorset
BH1Z 4AD

Silk embroidery and lace thread

E. and J. Piper
Silverlea
Flax Lane
Glemsford, Suffolk
C010 7RS

Silk weaving yarn

Hilary Chetwynd
Kipping Cottage
Cheriton
Alresford
Hants
SO24 0PW

Frames and mounts

Doreen Campbell
'Highcliff'
Bremilham Road
Malmesbury
Wilts

Matt coloured transparent adhesive film

Heffers Graphic Shop
26 King Street
Cambridge
CB1 1LN

United States of America

Arbor House
22 Arbor Lane
Roslyn Hights
NY 11577

Baltazor Inc.
3262 Severn Avenue
Metairie
LA 7002

Beggars' Lace
P.O. Box 17263
Denver
Colorado 80217

Berga Ullman Inc.
P.O. Box 918
North Adams
Massachusetts 01247

Frederick J. Fawcett
129 South Street
Boston
Massachusetts 02130

Frivolite
15526 Densmore N.
Seattle
Washington 98113

Happy Hands
3007 S.W. Marshall
Pendleton
Oregon 97180

International Old Lacers
P.O. Box 1029
Westminster
Colorado 80030

Lace Place de Belgique
800 S.W. 17th Street
Boca Raton
FL 33432

Lacis
2150 Stuart Street
Berkeley
California 9470

Robin's Bobbins
RTL Box 1736
Mineral Bluff
Georgia 30559

Robin and Russ Handweavers
533 North Adams Street
McMinnvills
Oregon 97128

Some Place
2990 Adline Street
Berkeley
California 94703

Osma G. Todd Studio
319 Mendoza Avenue
Coral Gables
Florida 33134

The Unique And Art Lace
  Cleaners
5926 Delman Boulevard
St Louis
Missouri 63112

Van Scriver Bobbin Lace
130 Cascadilla Park
Ithaca
New York 14850

The World in Stitches
82 South Street
Milford
N.H. 03055

Australia

Dentelles Lace Supplies
3 Narrak Close
Jindalee
Queensland 4074

The Lacemaker
94 Fordham Avenue
Hartwell
Victoria 3124

Spindle and Loom
Arcade 83
Longueville Road
Lane Cove
NSW 2066

Tulis Crafts
201 Avoca Street
Randwick
NSW 2031

Belgium

't Handwerkhuisje
Katelijnestraat 23
8000 Bruges
Belgium

Kantcentrum
Balstraat 14
8000 Bruges

Manufacture Belge de
  Dentelle
6 Galerie de la Reine
Galeries Royales St Hubert
1000 Bruxelles

Orchidee
Mariastraat 18
8000 Bruges

France

Centre d'Initiation à la
  Dentelle du Puy
2 Rue Duguesclin
43000 Le Puy en Velay

A L'Econome
Anne-Marie Deydier
Ecole de Dentelle aux
  Fuseaux
10 rue Paul Chenavard
69001 Lyon

Rougier and Ple
13–15 bd des Filles de
  Calvaire
75003 Paris

West Germany

Der Fenster Laden
Berliner Str 8
D 6483 Bad Soden
Salmunster

P.P. Hempel
Ortolanweg 34
1000 Berlin 47

Heikona De Ruijter
Kloeppelgrosshandel
Langer Steinweg 38
D4933 Blomberg

Holland

Blokker's Boektiek
Bronsteeweg 4/4a
2101 AC Heemstede

Theo Brejaart
Postbus 5199
3008 AD Rotterdam

Magazijn *De Vlijt*
Lijnmarkt 48
Utrecht

Switzerland

Fadehax
Inh. Irene Solca
4105 Biel-Benken
Basel

New Zealand

Peter McLeavey
P.O. Box 69.007
Auckland 8

Sources of Information

The Lace Guild
The Hollies
53 Audnam
Stourbridge
West Midlands
DY8 4AE

The Lace Society
Linwood
Stratford Road
Oversley
Alcester
Warwickshire
BY9 6PG

The British College of Lace
21 Hillmorton Road
Rugby
Warwickshire
CV22 5DF

The English Lace School
Honiton Court
Rockbeare
Nr Exeter
Devon

International Old Lacers
President
Gunvor Jorgensen
366 Bradley Avenue
Northvale
NJ 076647
United States

United Kingdom Director of
  International Old Lacers
S. Hurst
4 Dollius Road
London
N31 RG

Ring of Tatters
Mrs C. Appleton
Nonesuch
5 Ryeland Road
Ellerby
Saltburn by Sea
Cleveland TS13 5LP

Index

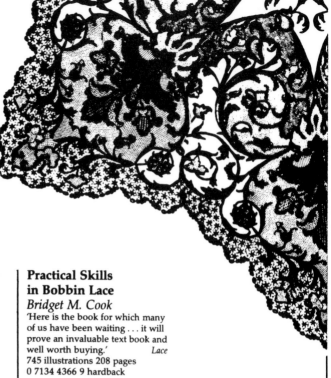